Plain
SPEAKING

PHIL LINEHAN
❖ ❖ ❖

A Reporter's Conversations with
President George W. Bush and Prime Minister
Tony Blair's Conversations with Wife Cherie

ISBN: 1-4196-9177-5
ISBN-13: 9781419691775

Visit www.booksurge.com to order additional copies.

TABLE OF CONTENTS

A British newspaper reporter posted to Washington just before the war in Iraq, I attended President Bush's press conferences when he often mentioned his close friend and collaborator, Tony Blair. For his part, in Britain the Prime Minister made frequent references to his ally and how they stood shoulder to shoulder. There was also much talk about their special relationship. Like others, I was curious to know how two people with apparently so little in common, and who, more often than not, did not seem to be speaking the same language, could have such empathy. It never occurred to me I would become privy to details of what took place when they conferred.

At presidential press conferences I was lucky to be called upon to put a few questions to the President, causing envy among some American colleagues who always seemed to be overlooked. It became obvious Mr. Bush was having interpretation problems when, after he answered one of my questions, his press secretary told me he had been instructed to invite me to visit the White House. He could give me no reason for the invitation. All he could suggest was that the President might want me to "explain the Brits". Flattered, I readily accepted. I had the privilege of being invited back time and time again for what the President called "our little chats" that covered a wide range of subjects far removed from linguistic differences.

It was not my intention to publish my notes on what the President and I discussed but, on reflection, I decided doing so would offer a glimpse into the thought processes of the two leaders before and during the early days of the Iraq war. As many of those mentioned in my notes, including Mr. Blair, have now left the scene and the time approaches when Mr. Bush must step down, the record I kept of the conversations might be of assistance to future historians. As it seemed that neither ever quite grasped what the other really meant, it might also help to explain some of their decisions. What was said between the President and me is as written. My interpretation of how Mr. Blair and his wife Cherie discussed his talks with Mr. Bush are based on information given to me by some of their close associates. I have been assured that, while not verbatim, my reconstructions very closely reflect exchanges between the then Prime Minister and his wife. Special thanks are due to Mr. Alastair Campbell, for so long Mr. Blair's Press Secretary and Chief Spinner, whose comments to and about the press, both on and off the record, were always illuminating.

My meetings with the President took place in a small private study off the Oval Office.

1. Foreign Affairs

Good morning, Mr. President. Thank you for inviting me to the White House.

Good morning. Glad to see you again. That press conference went well, didn't it? Sometimes I find the Brits a bit hard to understand because of the funny way they say things, but I have never had any problems with you, That's why I asked you to come here. To see if you can help me out with some of the things Tony tells me.

Mr. Blair, Sir? I thought you understood one another very well.

Sure we do but I don't always get what he means and you might be able to set me straight. But before we talk about Tony I'd like your take on foreign affairs. I want to be remembered as the president who really got the hang of what's happening in countries with all those strange names.

As you wish, Sir, but my American press colleagues seem to think there are a few pressing domestic matters that need your urgent attention. The economy, unemployment, affirmative action......

We'll talk about all that some other time. What about this Osama bin Laden guy. We haven't caught him yet, have we?

No, sir, he's proving to be very elusive. They still have not discovered where he is.

Well, now, I had a very senior CIA man here the other day who told me he was probably hiding out in the Indian crush. It took me a while to get what he meant but then it made sense. There are an awful lot of Indians. I saw TV pictures of a place called Mumbai and it was chock full of people, bumping into one another. And the trains, people sitting on the roofs and clinging to the sides. Anyone could go unnoticed in that crush.

Mr. President, Mumbai is what used to be called Bombay, but I think you may have misheard what the CIA man said.

No. I sometimes forget exactly what people say so I try to picture what they are talking about, like the comics with bubbles coming out of their mouths, or the top of their heads. While he was talking

I distinctly recall seeing lots of guys in turbans, obviously Indians.

You use mnemonics but that can be misleading. In this case I think he might have said bin Laden was hiding out in the Hindu Kush. It seems a likely place.

Well I can tell you I find those nem things very useful. But what kind of a place is a kush? Some kind of temple? And they say he's a Muslim so why would he hide in a Hindu one? Don't they have any Muslim kushes where he'd feel more at home?

The Hindu Kush is an area that is part in Pakistan and part in Afghanistan. There probably aren't too many Hindus there.

Then we should go after him there. Didn't someone say we would get him dead or alive?

I believe that was you Sir.

No, you can't pull that one on me. You all seem to forget I'm a Yale man and someone told me there's no better example of the kind of education you can get at Yale. So I know there's no way I could get him, or anyone else for that matter, if I was dead.

I think, Sir, the phrase dead or alive referred to the pursu-ee rather than the pursu-er.

And is Osama the ee or the er?

He would be the ee Sir.

Well then, we should tell the CIA to stop looking on Indian train roofs and head for that cushy spot you mentioned. But the one that's really bugging me is Saddam Hussein. He's the one in Iraq, isn't he? Not Iran? It's very confusing with names so similar.

They used to have other names. Iraq, or part of it, used to be Mesopotamia and Iran reminds us of Persia.

I never knew Black Jack was in Iran. I know he was in Mexico and the Philippines and Europe. But all the way over there? What a guy!

No, Sir, General Pershing never got that far. I said Persia, now Iran.

Well, well, don't we just learn something every day! I once spent hours looking at maps to find the country where the car-

pets come from and five minutes with you and I can stick a pin in it. But let's get back to Saddam. He's the one that tried to kill my dad and I have no doubt he'll try to kill me too.

I'm glad you can pinpoint the carpet country. Indeed you did say Saddam Hussein tried to kill your father but that's something that puzzles me. You see, Sir, American presidents have always been killed by Americans.

Is that a fact? You mean you've got to be a citizen before you can kill an American president? I never knew that, is it a law, or is it in the Constitution?

No, Sir, it just happens that way.

So it's a tradition, is it? Well, that's a comfort. We just won't let him become a citizen when he applies and that will get rid of that problem. Now what are we going to do about North Korea? Things seem to be getting out of hand there. I saw those crowds in the streets shouting and making all kinds of anti-American demonstrations.

They were South Koreans, Sir.

Aren't they supposed to be on our side?

Yes, they are. But they don't like American servicemen killing their teenagers and then getting away with it.

Well, all I can say is, they should try to be more reasonable. They should remember we're their friends. Meanwhile, the other Koreans seem to be piling up nucular – I can never say that darn word – weapons. They might use them and we can't let that happen, can we? Have any countries ever used weapons like that?

Only one, Sir.

Well, come on, which one was it?

The United States.

We were the only ones? You mean no-one ever tried to compete with us?

No, Sir. So far no other country has joined the league and we can only hope they never do.

2. The Lay of the Land

Good morning, Mr. President.

Good morning, glad to see you. I saw another of those Lou Dobbs news shows where they keep on and on about how many Enron people have been charged. I wish they'd lay off Kenneth Lay. The poor guy must be suffering enough without having to listen to that.

I don't think they're concerned about how many have been charged. I believe it's the ones who haven't been charged that causes the concern. And their viewers seem to agree with them.

Anyway, it's a darn shame. I hardly watch TV any more. The only thing worth seeing is that Osbournes show. I used to watch Martha Stewart but I can't get her now. I wonder why?

Well, Mr. President, she doesn't appear because of her insider trading problems. She's facing the same scrutiny as your friend Kenny Boy.

Now you know that name's on the list.

Sorry, I forgot about the list of forbidden names. I'm afraid Miss Stewart and Mr. Lay are now both in bad odour.

I can't believe what you're saying. Where did that come from? I haven't heard any-thing about it. And I'm supposed to have the best intelligence.

I beg your pardon. Oh you must mean the best intelligence services. But it's common knowledge and has been for some time.

Well, I can't find words to express my in-dignation. How could they be so dumb? And there's poor Linda selling second-hand clothes to make ends meet.

Mr. President, you mean Mrs. Lay holds yard sales?

What kind of a question is that? You can't hold yard sales in a mansion. She got someone to give her what used to be a pet shop where she sells used things she no longer wants. Laura got a friend to have a look, without saying who sent her of course. Most things are quite pricey but there are bargains to be had if you look

*carefully. We picked up some nice flat-
ware, monogrammed.*

Won't people notice that the initials are
not yours, Sir?

*Oh, it's not for us. It's a wedding present
for a daughter of friends of ours who has
the same initials. But getting back to this
scandal about Lay and Stewart. Why
did they have to do it? Martha Stewart
comes from up north, doesn't she, so she
must have a log cabin in the woods somewhere. They could have gone there and
nobody would have been any the wiser.*

Sir, I'm afraid you've lost me. Why would
Kenneth Lay and Martha Stewart want to
go to a log cabin?

*Wouldn't it be more discreet than sneak-
ing off to that place you mentioned, Bad
something-or-other, which must be one
of those German spas, where they could
easily be recognised? I bet they have television there too.*

I was talking about their reputations.

*And serves them darn well right. In my
opinion their behaviour is absolutely outra-*

geous. Poor Linda, although I can't phone her, I must find a way to let her know I feel for her.

3. Oh! Canada

Good morning, Mr. President.

Good morning. There's something that's really bothering me.

What would that be, Sir?

It's this problem we're having with the Canadians. They've been making a heck of a fuss about the little mishap with our boys when they bombed and killed their soldiers. Now I know they're our good neighbours, and they export a lot of comedians to the United States but it was friendly fire, after all, so why all the to-do? It wasn't as if they meant it.

No, the Canadians didn't like it one bit. What they particularly didn't like was when they found out that the U.S. flyers bombing them were on speed.

Well, wouldn't they have to be? I was only in the Texas National Guard during Vietnam (my dad fixed that) but I know that war planes are meant to have speed; otherwise they would be sitting ducks.

They would indeed, Sir. That is if ducks could sit in the air. Oh, my God! It's contagious.

You know I won't have the Lord's name taken. What's contagious?

Nothing, Mr. President. The mention of ducks made me think of those poor California chickens and the contagious exotic Newcastle disease they are now suffering from. But to get back to the Canadians, it wasn't the kind of speed you mean. It was the amphetamine type. Pills that get you so revved up they make you feel you are master of the universe and can do no wrong. The Air Force calls them go pills. And they've been used before, in Afghanistan when a lot of people, about 40 it was reported, were bombed and killed at a wedding party.

What, 40 Afghans?

They're dogs.

I don't think you should say that whatever you think. People would take you for a racist and you know what kind of trouble that can cause. I don't want to subject of race ever to be mentioned or we might get into all that crap about affirmative action and quotas and so on.

What I meant, Sir, is that to avoid confusion we now try to remember to call the people Afghanis since the hounds are afghans.

Nobody ever told me that. But getting back to the pills, isn't it illegal to use them?

Indeed it is, Sir.

You mean our forces are using illegal drugs?

Yes, I'm afraid they are. And not only the go pills. They also use no go pills.

What are they?

They slow you down, make you almost comatose.

Well, then, isn't it just common sense to make our boys take one of each and then here wouldn't be a problem. In any case, where do they get them from if they're illegal?

I don't really know. Perhaps the military train their own traffickers and pushers. If I may make a suggestion, Sir, perhaps that is something about which you might consult members of your family to bring you up to speed.

4. Me and My Shadow

Good Morning, Mr. President.

Good morning. I had a call from London today, from Tony. I wish he wasn't called Tony. Except for his accent, I think I'm talking to someone from the Sopranos instead of a president or a head of state.

Mr. Blair is neither president nor head of state.

Gee, that's too bad, is there anything we could do to get the Brits to make him head of state? It might give him a bit of tone. Ha, ha, that's pretty neat isn't it? Give Tony some tone. And I'm told many say I have no sense of humour.

It's hilarious. But they already have a head of state. A queen.

Wow! You don't say! A queen as head of state and everyone knows about it and they don't care? So they also have "don't ask, don't tell"?

Not that kind of queen, sir. A woman, with a crown and a court and lots of jewels. But she can't travel much because she has to stay at home and try to keep some kind of order in her family.

Why? Can't she get a nanny to look after them? I hear the English ones are very good.

It's not quite so simple. In the old days, before there was TV, kings and other royalty used to keep jesters at Court for their entertainment. Now in England the royal family are the jesters and the people keep them for their amusement. So there has to be someone in charge.

I'm glad you told me that so next time Tony comes I can ask him about the Queen, the Crown and the Court.

Well, Mr. President, I don't think that would be advisable. Just now the Crown and the Court, although another kind of court, are sore subjects and he might misunderstand your question.

Well then, maybe I can ask him about that exotic place you mentioned the other day. Newcastle. I don't know why that reminds me of firewood.

It should remind you of coal.

I knew it was something hot. But maybe I won't say anything. He might think it's tactless now that they've got that contagious disease. In any case, I always enjoy Tony's visits. He's got some great qualities. He never argues, always agrees with me and does whatever I ask him to do. That's why I make sure to keep him jumping through the hoop as they say.

Keep him in the loop, I think is the expression, Sir.

Whatever. Besides, I learn a lot from him, new words and expressions, almost another language. The other day I told him something funny and he said I'd pickled him pink.

You tickled him.

I did nothing of the kind. We're chums but we're not that chummy.

I see what you mean about the new language. And it's great that you get on so well. It must be a relief not to have an interpreter present. The conversation must flow better.

Yeah, we do hit it off. Once when I told him something he hadn't heard he said I could have knocked him up with a feather.

You could have knocked him down.

Now why would I want to do a darned fool thing like that? Didn't I say we're friends? Besides, although I'm in great shape, I think he's a bit younger than me, or at least he says he is, so he might have the advantage.

I'm sorry Sir, I don't know what I was thinking of.

Then there was the time I told him about Kenneth Lay and Martha Stewart and he was so surprised he said it was a real turnip for the cooks.

It was a turn up for the books.

Oh, well, that too, if you say so.

Obviously, Mr. President, Mr. Blair is someone who has your confidence and it is clear that you get more out of his visits than just learning a new language,

You can say that again. He always brings me one of those little black jars of Marmite.

5. Explosive Issues

Good morning, Mr. President.

Good morning, it's good to see you. I'm getting really worried about Tony. His hair seems to be receding and his behaviour has become very odd.

I'm sorry Mr. Blair is losing his hair.

I told him to massage olive oil into his scalp every day. It works for me. For some reason he didn't seem too pleased. But what's causing me great concern is his odd behaviour.

I'm surprised. He always gives the impression of behaving quite normally.

Then how do you explain his sudden concern about the egg market.

I'm afraid I don't understand Sir. I thought you said the egg market. Do you mean the hedge market? A lot of people are concerned about it. If he's put money in it, he's right to be worried.

If I meant the hedge market I would have said so. Why do people always think I don't know what I'm talking about? The egg market. You know, those things we couldn't eat because they were full of cholesterol and now they've found a way to pump it out, so we can eat them again. Eggs.

Oh, sorry. I have to confess I never really gave much thought to the egg market. I should think Mr. Blair has other things to worry about. How did the subject come up?

That's what's so strange. The other day, while we were discussing Iraq and North Korea, I was told Don Rumsfeld was on the phone and I went into the other room to talk to him. He said he'd just heard his German relations had disowned him.

That must have come as a shock.

Yeah, I guess so. He said he couldn't think why. When I mentioned it to Tony he started asking about the price of eggs and what I was doing about it. I know nothing about the price of eggs. Laura is the one who goes to the supermarket. I haven't got time. For a moment I thought he meant the Commodities Market. I don't know why Tony is so concerned with the price of eggs. He must get a good salary; I know his wife earns a lot. They have a great house in the centre of London and a country place. And if the price of eggs has risen it's probably due to that disease they sent us from Newcastle that's affecting our California chickens. So in his place I'd keep quiet about it.

I think what Mr. Blair probably said, referring to Mr. Rumsfeld's family problems, was "what has that got to do with the price of eggs?" It means that what you said has nothing to do with anything. In other words, it's irrelevant.

All I can say is that as an Englishman he should be more careful about how he uses the language.

Actually, Sir, Mr. Blair was born in Scotland.

That explains it then. It's not his language so no wonder he gets mixed up.

Mr. Blair has been in England a long time and when children learn a foreign language at a very young age they learn it well. So I think we can assume he feels quite at home with English.

I've always been against sending kids off to school in foreign countries. It affects them later in life. But eggs are the least of it. He's using language I simply won't tolerate. I told him we were fixing to have a barbecue at Camp David, a mixed one. First of all he said it was a good idea because if it wasn't mixed people might accuse me of discriminating against minorities. I set him straight on that by explaining that by a mixed barbecue I meant we'd not only have spare ribs, my favourite, but other cuts and even sausages for those who wanted them. You know what he said?

I couldn't even begin to guess, Sir.

I can hardly bring myself to repeat it. He said there's nothing he enjoys more than a good bang. Now, as you know I'm not a prude, in fact some accuse me of being too tolerant, but I thank my lucky stars there was so much noise with all the people there that Laura didn't hear.

I'm sure he said he likes nothing more than a good banger, which is what English sausages are called.

Now why on earth would sausages be called bangers?

Because they explode.

Good grief! Exploding sausages! And do they have those exploding sausages in London?

They have them all over the country. The people love them.

Well, I'll really have to rethink my buddy-buddy act with Tony. I must remember to get the FBI to pass me his file. Here he drops in as if he owns the place and now you tell me his country is full of exploding sausages. I find that very suspicious, especially after they tried to send us that guy with exploding shoes.

Sir, I don't think the sausages hurt anyone, except perhaps those who eat them.

The sausages probably explain why they threw everyone out of Gatwick airport when they found explosives in a British Airways plane.

No explosives were found in a plane, Sir. A passenger was taking his suitcase out of the airport when it was checked by Customs and they found a grenade in it.

Well then, wasn't clearing the airport like locking the stable door after the horse has bolted?

Yes, it was Sir, but it made great headlines.

That just shows you. That Hussein guy will stop at nothing.

The passenger was a Venezuelan citizen and there is no indication so far that he has anything to do with Iraq.

I can see the connection even if you can't. I know a little bit about oil and there's oil in Venezuela just as there is in Iraq. What more proof do you want? And what about the alarm at Heathrow when they sent tanks into the streets? I can't agree with that.

Oh, so you too think it was an overreaction. A lot of people think the same.

I don't know anything about an overreaction. What I want to know is how they expected to get the tanks through the revolving doors at Heathrow.

Tony's conversation with Cherie

Hello, Tony. I didn't expect you back so soon. What happened?

We left a little earlier than planned.

Is anything wrong? You look quite drawn. I think these constant trips to Washington are getting you down.

God, I need a drink. What's getting me down is George. He's acting very strange, the things he says are quite inconsequential. At times I simply don't understand a word.

For example?

First of all he implied that I'm thin on top and told me to rub salad oil or something into my scalp. You don't think I'm losing my hair do you?

Of course not. What an idea! Although you might try combing it a bit towards the front. But let's get back to George's behaviour.

Well, we were talking about our war, as we usually do. He went to the other room to take a phone call and came back muttering something about Donald Rumsfeld's German relations. In the scheme of things I thought that was pretty irrelevant and I couldn't resist saying so.

And that upset him?

No, apparently it didn't. In fact, I doubt if he even heard me because he suddenly said he knew nothing about the commodities market. Now, I ask you, what had that got to do with anything?

Maybe your remark made him want to distract you from Rumsfeld. He's not a subject many people care to dwell on. Maybe he was concerned about the effect the war that you and he are planning would have on commodities.

Surely if he had any worries about the market it would be the one on Wall Street. But that's not the worst thing that happened.

Go on, I'm all agog,

He said he was arranging a barbecue at Camp David, a mixed one. Because of all the to-do about Trent Lott and the Republican Party being a white men's club, I thought he meant there would be a range of skin tones among the guests.

You mean a motley crowd?

Exactly. But no, he explained they were going to serve mixed cuts, sausages and so on. I distinctly remember he said spare ribs were his favourite. Just to make small talk I said I, on the other hand, liked sausages. You'll never believe what happened.

Not unless you tell me I won't.

He sort of went berserk. He glared at me and started shouting "where's Laura, where's Laura". I tell you it was chilling.

How did the others react?

Fortunately we were a bit apart and there was a good deal of noise with so many guests. Laura was nowhere to be seen.

That must have really upset him.

The odd thing is that when he couldn't see her, instead of being more alarmed, he calmed down. Frankly, I began to suspect he was having an attack of the D.T.'s. But then I realized it couldn't be that because he doesn't, that is he can't, drink any more. So then I thought it might be a D.W.S.

What's a D.W.S? A Demented War Syndrome?

Cherie, please try not to be facetious. It's Delayed Withdrawal Syndrome. He then drew me aside, said he understood all about urges and went babbling on about having to be very careful about what we say in mixed company.

So that was the worst thing?

No, there's more. A propos of absolutely nothing, he repeated what he had told me the last time I was with him, a most scabrous piece of gossip about Kenneth Lay and Martha Stewart.

Gossip? Now we're getting to the best part. Come on, out with it.

He said he had it from a very reliable source that they'd gone off together and were in Bad Oder, which I suppose is a spa in Brandenburg near the River Oder. If I remember my geography that's right on the Polish border isn't it?

That makes perfect sense. Martha Stewart is not, as you might imagine, one of your fellow Scots. She is really the Polish Martha Kostyra so she must have chosen the place. If things got too hot for them, they could easily slip cross the border.

Oh for heaven's sake, we're getting as bad as he is. I'm sure there's no truth whatsoever in the story. In fact, I put out a few feelers, just asking what was the latest about Martha Stewart, and nobody mentioned anything like that although, now that I come to think of it, they did say she was in hot water. I'm really starting to wonder if old George is losing it, going a bit bonkers with the strain of not being able to put the Marines into Baghdad right away. He thought his Blitzkrieg would be over by now. What do you think?

About the Blitzkrieg or about him losing it? If it's the latter then I think you can put your mind at rest. There's simply no way that George Bush can be losing it.

It's a relief to hear you say that, but why are you so sure?

My dear Tony, you know just as well as I do that one can't possibly lose it if one hasn't got it!

6. The French Disconnection

Good morning, Mr. President. You must be glad that the invasion of Iraq is under way at last.

Good morning. Yeah, we finally did it although a day later than I wanted. I wanted it to start on the 17th but I was told it would interfere with the St. Patrick's Day celebrations. But it's not an invasion, it's a liberation. We call it Operation Iraqi Freedom.

Yes, Sir, of course, I forgot. Besides Iraq, I see you have had a very full agenda what with your trip to the Azores and so on. That must have been exhausting but, if I may say so, you look extremely well.

Lots of people say that. It's the old adrenaline. The Azores thing only lasted an hour but it gave me a chance to get to know the Spanish President, José Aznar, a bit better. I'd like to get your take on him, maybe when we get together again.

I look forward to that. But Mr. Aznar is not the Spanish president. He is not head of state but president of the government which is a kind of chairman of all the ministers, so he is really Prime Minister.

First you say Blair isn't a president and now Aznar. Aren't there any presidents over there I could talk to?

Yes there is one, Sir, but I don't think you're on speaking terms at the moment. His name is Jacques Chirac and he's President of France.

It's exactly the French I want to talk about. It bugs me that I can't hit them hard. We've tried, mind you. You've probably heard we no longer have French toast, it's now freedom toast. And in California they threw hundred of gallons of French wine, Beaujolais I think, down the drains.

I know you'd like to get back at the French but why only them? The Germans and the Russians are being just as awkward.

We thought about the Germans but it's really too much to ask the American people to give up their hamburgers or their frankfurters. What else is there, except German measles?

To really blast the Germans perhaps you could give serious thought to sending Mr. Donald Rumsfeld back to them.

Do you think they'd accept him? After all, even his own relations in Germany don't want him.

Oh, I think they'd have to. In Germany nationality is based on ancestry. Of all the people who have ever mentioned Mr. Rumsfeld to me not one has ever expressed the slightest doubt when mentioning his ancestry.

Well, I'll have to think about it. As to the Russians, I'm glad to say that one was easy to deal with. I had the word spread among the casino operators that they should no longer let their customers play Russian roulette.

Mr. President, you constantly astonish me. I would give anything to be a fly on the wall and see Mr. Putin's face when he learns about that.

Yeah, that would sure as heck be a sight to see, wouldn't it?

Getting back to the French. I believe the efforts you've made so far won't really have much effect. In fact, they can be either counterproductive or they might leave the French totally bewildered.

What do you mean?

Take the wine, for example. I can think of nothing that would gladden the heart of a wine producer more than seeing people pay good money for his product just to pour it down the drain. That must be a wine producer's dream, especially now that there's a glut. The French fries are actually Belgian and, as to French toast, it's unknown in France.

What do they eat for breakfast?

They eat what they call croissants and the rest of the day they eat baguettes. I don't think the French palate is one that would appreciate soggy fried bread. Besides, if you start with toast you have to go on to so many other things like French horns, French dressing, French beans, French doors or windows, French pastry, French kiss.....

Yeah, yeah, I get the point. Only the other day poor Laura was in a terrible state trying to tell me something without using the "F" word. Finally, when I couldn't understand what the heck she was on about she blurt-ed out "Oh, for goodness sake, I've got to hire a French polisher". It's hard. Can't you suggest anything?

I do have an idea but it would mean asking the American people to make a great sacrifice,

War is a time for sacrifices. I'm sure the American people would be happy to do whatever we ask them. So what's your idea?

I thought you might call upon everyone who has them – and I imagine it's a very large proportion of the population – to put all their French letters into large envelopes and address them to Mr. Chirac.

That's one great idea but I don't think it would work. He'd only get some of his henchmen to read them for him.

Yes, of course, I hadn't thought of that. But you must remember, if you don't mind my saying so, here we are dealing with a case totally different from Germany and Russia. I believe only a gesture on a very grand scale would impress the French.

I'm afraid you're right. I can't stand the way that guy Chirac always seems to be

looking down on everyone. He's looks so smug and superior.

That's because he is.

He is what?

Oh, smug, Sir. Yes, definitely smug.

O.K. so what's your bright idea about how we might screw the French?

It is something I have been pondering and I believe I've hit on what we might call revenge in the grand manner. I've learned that the manufacturers of duct tape have been going all out, three shifts I've been told, to make enough to seal all the houses, offices and other buildings in the United States. Maybe you could ask them to go the extra mile and make a batch big enough to wrap the Statue of Liberty and send it back to France, to Paris where it came from. I haven't the slightest doubt that such a gesture would really make an impression on them. And, to make an even bigger impact, if I were you, Mr. President, I'd ask my people to make sure to send it C.O.D

7. Hail the Conquering Hero

Good morning Mr. President.

Good morning. When we last met I said I wanted you to tell me about José Aznar. He seems quite an interesting guy. Very upbeat.

He is probably still basking in the glory of his country's victory at the Battle of Parsley Island.

I'm glad you mentioned that. Just as I was leaving for the Azores, one of my advisers told me to ask him about parsley. I thought that, for once, I might have misunderstood. There suddenly seems to be an awful lot of talk about food. First Tony Blair goes on about eggs and then my guys asked me to talk to José Aznar about parsley. I was beginning to wonder if I was missing something.

No, Mr. President, you were not mistaken. The reference was to Isla del Perejil, known in English as Parsley Island, which is just off the Moroccan coast, close to Spain, and claimed by the Spaniards.

What of it? Did something happen there I should have been told about?

Last year the Moroccans invaded it and Mr. Aznar was forced to rally the country behind him, making thunderous proclamations of Spanish sovereignty over the territory and calling on the Spanish people to defend it whatever the cost. He said no steps would be spared to throw the invaders out. Many say it was his finest hour.

And did they succeed in getting rid of the invaders

Indeed they did. By mustering all the might of the Spanish armed forces, gunboats, submarines, attack helicopters, their special ground forces, they got rid of the Moroccans in very short order.

Wow! So they've got a great rapid response facility?

Yes, Sir. The operation only lasted a few hours until the Moroccans withdrew.

Well, I always knew the Spaniards could win great battles. I remember at school we learned about the battle of the Spanish Armada.

I don't think that would be a good subject to bring up with Mr. Aznar.

In any case, why on earth didn't my people tell me about the Battle of Parsley Island before? I could have asked José to get his generals to talk to ours. I suppose their helicopters were used to vertically envelop the key Moroccan positions?

I'm not sure about that. I don't think there were any key Moroccan positions.

What do you mean no key positions? The invaders must have been stationed somewhere.

I believe they just stood there.

How big an invasion force are we talking about?

There are conflicting reports on that. Some say they were six, others go as high as twelve.

It's no use giving me numbers unless you explain what they were. Battalions. divisions, platoons, units?

Definitely units, Sir.

Well what size were they?

All different sizes I should imagine.

Were there many casualties?

None, Mr. President. Neither on the Spanish side nor on the Moroccan side.

That's amazing. You mean not even casualties from friendly fire? Didn't the Moroccans use their weapons to resist?

I am sure they would have, if they'd had any.

How big is the territory? They tell me Iraq is about a quarter of a million miles.

Parsley Island is about one.

A million miles. I never knew there was an island that big near Spain.

No, Sir. It's the one that counts, not the million.

What about the inhabitants? Did they welcome being freed by the Spaniards, or are they Moroccans?

Their reaction can best be described as one of utter indifference. They are neither

Spaniards nor Moroccans. Actually, they are goats.

You don't say? But why aren't they called Parsleans if the country is Parsley Island?

I've no idea Sir. I do not believe anyone has ever given the matter any thought.

I have to say I find this all very strange. Are you sure you got it right?

Quite sure. If I seem to be rather vague it's because I have not been able to discover anything in the annals of military history to compare to the Battle of Parsley Island. So I'm finding it somewhat difficult to describe.

Well, maybe I won't bring it up with our military leaders. But I might ask State about it. They must have heard something and maybe they could fill me in on a few more details. There's one thing I'd like to know. How did the Moroccan forces get there, what landing craft did they use?

Again there are conflicting versions. Those who put the invading force at twelve units say they saw a few rowboats take off from the Moroccan coast. Those who say they numbered six, swear they stormed the

Parsley shores with half a dozen pedalos borrowed from a nearby amusement area where they were celebrating their King's marriage.

8. Plain Speaking

Good morning, Mr. President.

Good morning. How are you doin'?

I'm very well Sir. And if I may say so, every time I see you, you look more relaxed.

Yeah, I'm making sure I hit the hay promptly at 10 every night. You know Tony was here again on one of his flying visits. You won't believe this, but he keeps insisting on talking about food. It's true he looks very peaked and seems to be losing weight. I wonder if Cherie is giving him enough to eat?

I don't think it can be poor nutrition but maybe all the criticism he's facing at home is getting him down. You know a lot of people there are against the war. Some very prominent personalities in politics and even the Church have voiced their opposition.

It was just when I was telling him how sorry I was to hear the Archbishop of Canterbury was going to the Middle East to a meeting of Christian and Muslim religious leaders that he suddenly said he'd had enough taffy. Now I can assure you we never offer our visitors taffy. That would be tacky. And we're not like the Kennedy White House either. A friend of my dad's told me they used to give their guests some fancy things called little fours which, he said, came from you can guess where. I suppose they're called that because they're small and you only get four of them. We always give our visitors good old American cherry pie with ice cream. And we put no limit on the number of scoops,

I never knew the Kennedys offered little.... oh, I see, yes of course, petits fours do indeed originate in Old Europe so I can well understand your reluctance to offer them. As to the cherry pie, I'm sure Mr. Blair appreciated it. In fact, he mentioned it to the Press when he got home, but he said nothing about the number of ice cream scoops. He also mentioned, although nobody quite knows why, that you both use the same toothpaste.

That's a coincidence, isn't it? I guess he wanted to show how close we've become.

Yes indeed. But I believe I can explain the remark about taffy. He must have said

"I've had enough of that Taffy". You see, Sir, where Mr. Blair comes from a Welshman is called a Taffy, so he was saying he'd had enough of the Archbishop, Dr. Rowan Williams, who is Welsh.

It's a mighty funny thing to call a man of God. But that wasn't all. I was telling him that some people were beginning to wonder if Donald Rumsfeld should tone down his remarks when Tony said we didn't have enough sandwiches for a picnic. We don't go in for picnics, no siree, a good old barbecue is more to our taste. So again I didn't know what he was talking about.

I think I can also clarify that comment. Referring to Mr. Rumsfeld he must have said "he's one sandwich short of a picnic". He meant that in his considered opinion Mr. Rumsfeld does not have the cerebral endowments that one would hope for of someone in his position.

I'll take your word for it. What does it mean?

He's nuts. But it is odd that Mr. Blair used that expression. He would normally say something like "he's lost all his marbles" or "he's unhinged". Still, those phrases are now used by many people in Britain when they refer to their own Prime Minister so I suppose he's a bit sensitive about them. But I am sure you spoke of other things.

Oh we did. We talked about our faith, as we often do. I was delighted when I found out Tony is a believer. You never know with the Brits. Even though they have an official church, the Sea of something, they never seem to go to any services.

In England the people think the C. of E. as they call it, or the Church of England to give it the official name, is very handy for baptisms, weddings and funerals.

Now they shouldn't only use a place of worship every time they want to celebrate. No, I can't approve of that, as a born again Christian. Had you heard about that by any chance?

Yes, I had heard, Sir, many times. I understand you were born again at 40. But surely your mother objected, it must have been very hard on her?

Of course she didn't object, she was absolutely thrilled. She wished it had happened sooner.

Yes, I imagine she did. But getting back to Mr. Blair, it was a great surprise to his constituents when he came out of the closet.

What? You don't mean to tell me he's a....?

Oh, no, Mr. President, perish the thought. I mean when he came out of the closet as a Holy Roller. A British Prime Minister does not usually wear his religion on his sleeve or invoke God as a reason for invading and bombing a country. It is quite new to the British public to hear their leader declaiming about the morality of war.

Well, I don't want to brag but I believe I deserve some credit for that.

Nobody doubts that for a moment, Sir.

You know, I've been thinking about the problems I sometimes have in understanding Tony. I'm almost starting to wonder if we speak different languages.

I believe you may have something there, Sir. It seems the English language goes through a dramatic metamorphosis when it crosses the Atlantic, especially as it approaches Texas. But I see no reason why you should try to speak what is called the Queen's English. In fact, I've heard rumours there's a move afoot to make the President's English, or American rather, the official language of the United States.

Now, wouldn't that be just somethin'? Many people say I have a special way of using the language.

A second James Joyce.

What did he do?

In a certain way, he transformed the English language.

You know this guy? Could we get together with him to talk about words and so on?

I am afraid that would be difficult as he's no longer available for consultation. But I am absolutely convinced you need no help in transforming the language.

Maybe we could get rid of all those hard words my scriptwriters try to make me say.

You mean your speechwriters?

The ones who hand me little bits of paper and make me read from that proper thing.

Yes, Sir, a prompter can be a bit tricky, especially if it rolls too fast.

But if we did start to use the President's American, they'd have to add my name or people might think it was another president, maybe even a Democrat like Franklin Roosevelt.

I doubt that there would be any danger of your English being confused with President Roosevelt's, but they might think of the Republican President Eisenhower, whose use of the language was also quite singular, so adding your name would be a good idea.

Then, so that I can't be accused of discriminating against anyone, I could have the Muslim bible, what's it called?

The Koran

.... translated into the President's American and have a copy put in every hotel room so that everyone could clearly understand exactly what the Muslim religion is all about.

Tony's conversation with Cherie

Well, Tony, back again from another of your flying visits. I don't see why you always have to be the one hopping over the Atlantic if you are supposed to be equal partners. I can see he obviously thinks he's more equal than you are.

Oh, really, Cherie, stop harping. I'm not in the mood. Anyway, he has now agreed to come to Belfast. Another meeting I'm dreading. Bertie Ahern will be there too.

Is he getting involved in the war?

No, of course not. We'll be talking about the IRA and other matters concerning Northern Ireland. That's why we decided to invite the Irish Prime Minister.

It seems strange that George should be worrying about the IRA now when he must have other things on his mind. But was your trip less stressful this time?

No, if anything it was worse. He can't seem to stop talking about food. It's probably because he is always on a diet.

So what did he say?

I was telling him that I had just about enough of Rowan Williams when he suddenly started saying that the Kennedys never gave their guests enough to eat.

How odd. Of course it was before my time, but I've heard that they always did very well indeed by their guests with splendid banquets, gourmet food, the best wines from Old Europe with the odd Californian thrown in as a sop to the locals. So I wonder what he was talking about, and why go back so far?

I've no idea. But he gestured to a waiter to bring in some cherry pie. I mean really, can you imagine? Not only that, but another waiter brought in a huge dish of some revolting goo George said was ice cream. He kept shoving it at me and saying I could take as many scoops as I wanted.

Well, you're lucky the waiter didn't bring in a huge dish of chili con carne which, I am told, in Texas passes for haute cuisine.

I managed to put away a few scoops when he started talking about Donald

Rumsfeld again. His name always seems to come up. I said many people think he's not all there, which you know is true. Well, George then started extolling the virtues of barbecues. You remember the last time he went on about mixed barbecues?

Whatever could he have meant? Was that before or after the ice cream incident?

Oh, I don't remember, what does it matter anyway? Then he asked me about the Archbishop again and mentioned some Sea or other. But it can't be the Sea of Galilee because Williams is going to the Gulf, which is nowhere near it. Who knows? In any case, I told him I thought the Archbishop was off his rocker preaching that war is evil, it is wrong to kill innocent people and bomb public markets and a lot of other such rot. Now I ask you, what way is that for the head of a Christian Church to talk? That reminds me, George keeps on and on about being a born again Christian. He has told me that so many times now that I don't know whether each time he tells me he's talking about another rebirth, or if he's repeatedly talking about the same one.

You don't think it could be a case of multiple rebirths? I've never heard of anything like that. Perhaps we could ask that Italian doctor if it's possible.

If that wasn't enough, as soon as I got back I was bombarded by questions from the hacks all asking me what we had discussed. Now how the devil can I tell them when I have only the vaguest idea of what he's talking about? I was reduced to mentioning the cherry pie and ice cream, although I said nothing about the scoops. I also told them George and I use the same toothpaste. I can tell you I got a lot of very odd looks.

Yes, I've heard the reporters' bars were abuzz with quips about there perhaps being more to your special relationship than meets the eye. You know what? I've just had a great idea about Bertie Ahern. Maybe you could ask him to be present at all your talks with George.

No, that wouldn't be at all appropriate. As Irish Prime Minister he has nothing to do with the war. Besides, I don't think it would go down well with his voters if he did get involved.

No, you don't understand. I don't mean he should join the discussions but I thought he could act as interpreter. I'm sure he would be a great help to you both.

I suppose that's meant to be a joke? Although, come to think of it, perhaps it wouldn't be such a bad idea. It might help me with the reporters. But I don't think George would take well to the suggestion.

I don't know why, but I have a very strong suspicion he might welcome it. But, Tony, I have to confess there is something that's beginning to worry me. Your insistence that other people, including your pal George, are bonkers. You know it's very dangerous when someone begins to think he's the only sane one in the loony bin.

Honestly, Cherie, I don't know what you're getting at but, if the insinuation is what I think it is, then I don't like it. That's the last I want to hear of it.

All right, you'll hear no more about it from me. But let me tell you I would rather not be around when the men in the white coats come calling.

9. No Known Cure

Good morning, Mr. President.

Good morning. They tell me you've been in New York.

Yes, Sir. I felt I needed a break and as I love the theatre New York is really the best place to take a few days off. I also saw that film about Mr. Giuliani.

I think far too much a fuss has been made about him.

Well, after all he did present quite a re-assuring figure in the aftermath of 9/11. He seemed to be able to find the right words.

All I could see was that he was hogging the spotlight. Anyone would think he was president instead of me. And what about his private life? Women. I can't under-stand how the people put up with public figures that don't know how to behave themselves. Kennedy and Clinton for ex-ample. But that's the Democrats for you.

If I'm not mistaken, Sir, Mr. Giuliani is a Republican. And then you have Mr. Newt Gingrich, also a Republican, who was up to no good himself while he so assiduously pursued Mr. Clinton.

Yeah, he did that, didn't he? And he went after him too you know.

People seem to be ready to forgive their politicians an awful lot. I can even imagine a president who might be a hopeless drunk, an intimate associate of some of the country's biggest corporate swindlers, known for his abuse of substances, and who has a record for driving while under the influence, being forgiven for his behaviour.

Do you have any particular president in mind?

Not at all, Sir. The president I mention is just an example, a figment of my imagination. What I'm trying to point out is that most misbehaviour, including that of, if you'll forgive my language, a sexual nature, does not seem to bother voters. We should not forget that even virtuous President Carter told the public he had lust in his heart.

Now this is not a criticism, but not everyone understands you as well as I do and some might think you meant something else. So, I believe it would be best to be very careful about using those figments.

Sorry, Sir. I tend to get carried away. In future I shall keep a very tight rein on my figments.

What you said about Jimmy Carter. I never heard that.

You might have been told. But at that time you had not yet been born again, so maybe that's why you do not remember.

Do you think he still has it? Even though he's a Democrat I'm convinced he's a good Christian so I'd be glad to help him.

How could you do that, Sir?

You know, we've got great heart doctors in Houston. I could recommend him or even give him a note to take.

I'm very happy to tell you that President Carter's heart trouble was cured long ago. Fortunately, it is condition that can be cleared up very easily.

I'm sure glad to hear that. I hope you're right because heart lust sounds very serious to me.

I can assure you it isn't, Sir. But there is another condition that can affect a president and, when it does, it is deadly.

Oh, gee, what's that? I hope they've discovered some kind of vaccination they can give you against it.

It's called blood lust and so far there is neither a vaccination nor a cure.

Are you sure? What are the doctors called who cure blood diseases? I've no doubt we've got some of them in Houston too.

They are haematologists. But they are totally helpless against this scourge.

You mean if a president got it, he could die?

No, Sir, that is what is so peculiar about this particular disease and makes it so hard to cure. The person who has it does not die but it kills untold numbers of people thousands of miles from where he is, people who have never met him, seen him, or indeed do not even know who he is.

As I see it, the important thing is that the president wouldn't die, so that's all that matters, isn't it? But let's stop talking about sicknesses. Is there anything you'd like to ask me about?

It seems a lot of people wonder why you oppose the University of Michigan's programme of setting aside places for disadvantaged students. Is there any particular reason?

I don't understand why they are against me on that. I can't agree with letting kids get in to college who've got to have help because they couldn't get the number of marks needed. I think merit should be all that counts.

Excuse me for asking, Sir, but, didn't you get into Yale even though you fell somewhat short of its academic standards?

That was quite different; there was no nonsense about marks or tests. I got in under the C.C. Programme.

I never knew Yale operated a Cerebrally Challenged Programme.

Don't be silly. It's what known as the Chosen Children Programme. My dad fixed that. He was at Yale himself and still has a lot of influence there.

Your father seems to fix a great many things for you. A real handyman if ever there was one. And I see he was also your father before you were born again.

He sure was. He's been my dad ever since the day I was born for the very first time.

10. Wrap the Duct Tape Round Me

Good morning, Mr. President.

Good morning, good to see you again. Today I'd like to get your opinion on our homeland security plans.

As I really knew very little about the matter I had to look it up. Some things puzzle me, I must confess.

Any doubts you have, just ask me.

Thank you Sir. But first I would like to mention that I have heard of the meeting between Mr. David Blunkett, the British Home Secretary, and Mr. Tom Ridge, the Homeland Security Secretary, when Mr. Blunkett said they were standing shoulder to shoulder. As this is the same phrase used by Prime Minister Tony Blair when referring to you, Mr. President, elderly people in Britain are beginning to wonder if he and his Cabinet are not seeing too many old late night films about the Canadian Mounties.

Yeah, I wondered about that. I guess it's meant to show that nothing can separate us.

The British authorities are taking their own precautions to protect their homeland. Their citizens have been told they should always have at hand a plastic bag with spare clothes. In case of an alarm, they must take off all their garments and put the spare clothes on. It is not clear whether people are expected always to have the plastic bag with them. I imagine they are, otherwise there would not be much point. It would serve no purpose if they left their spare clothes at home while they were at work, in a restaurant or cinema, or even on their way to work on the underground, that is the subway, when an alarm sounded.

I never heard that about the clothes. Maybe it could be added to our list. I suppose it's got to be done as quick as possible?

A time of three minutes has been set which, I have been told on good authority, has caused quite a lot of alarm and despondency among the less agile and arthritic members of the public.

Who decided it had to be three minutes?

It seems it was Home Secretary himself. I'm also told it was he who personally organized the "take it all off" trials at the Home Office.

How did that work?

All the personnel, from the most senior to the most junior, were ordered to assemble in a very large shed, plastic bags with spare clothes in hand, whip off all their clothes and put on the spares in the shortest possible time.

Dave Blunkett too?

Oh no, the Home Secretary did not disrobe. The supervision was done by one of his deputies who stood on a podium with stopwatch in hand to check the times. Assistants or monitors had also been placed throughout the shed. Mr. Blunkett was there to act as a kind of master of ceremonies.

You mean a cheerleader?

Something like that. The scene was described to me as at first being rowdy, then unruly and even uproarious with, I am sorry to have to report, quite a few ribald remarks flying around when staff members saw their colleagues in the altogether for the first time.

I hope Dave was able to get them to behave themselves.

Yes, he was, Sir, but it was no easy task. It seems it took many attempts before the three minute figure was reached, by which time it is said the situation had descended into one that can only be described as utter mayhem. A cleaning lady wanted to know how taking her knickers off would help to prevent terrorism. A Probation Service guard quipped that he knew of no better way to dishearten any terrorist. Then, from the back of the shed, came the frivolous suggestion that running the garment in question up the flagpole would be an even greater deterrent. I was told this caused so much merriment, as the lady concerned is decidedly stout and the garment, therefore, very voluminous, that the situation was getting quite out of control.

Poor Dave must have felt very disturbed.

No doubt. However, order was restored when a senior member of the Anti-Social Behaviour Unit joined Mr. Blunkett and called on everyone to act like adults. His exhortation was rather undermined because, while he had already stripped, he had not put on his spare clothes before he leaped onto the podium. Still, eventually they were all able to pull themselves together and concentrate on the task at hand. Finally some remarkable times were recorded, the best performer being a young Communications Service computer operator who whipped off her garments and put on the spares in an astounding 21 seconds. It was so unbelievable that I am told Mr. Blunkett's deputy and his assistants asked her to repeat it time and time again, just to make sure their stopwatches were right. I understand contact has already been made with the Guinness Book of Records.

That's incredible. So if they can do it that fast, why did they pick three minutes?

Well, Sir, sad to say, the Passport Service, never known for speed of action, really let the side down by taking an average of ten and a half minutes. When they had finished, Mr. Blunkett added up all the times taken by everyone, divided the result by the number he first thought of, and came up with the three minutes.

I must get Tom Ridge at Homeland Security to call Dave and congratulate him.

I am sure that would be much appreciated. As to your Homeland Security Department, I see it is not expected to be operational until the end of the year, at the very earliest, and it might take much longer to get off the ground. Are your people advising the terrorists that they must hold off any attacks until then?

Gee, I don't know. If they don't attack us in the meantime maybe it's better if it never gets off the ground. What do you think?

That's the opinion I believe a lot of people hold. But I have no doubt that eventually it, together with its 170,000 staff, will be up and running. We can only hope they do not trip over one another. But there are a few other things about it I don't understand. For example, the advice that everyone should seal all windows, doors and vents in what they decide is to be their secure hiding place, with duct tape and plastic sheeting. As I read it, this means that everything must be sealed so tightly that absolutely nothing can get in during the three days it is expected they will stay there. I was surprised to find no mention of keyholes. Might they not present a danger? The very fact that they are apertures through which things can pass.

Gosh, our boys definitely slipped up there. I'll see those responsible are dealt with. Anything else?

Yes. If the seals work as well as they should, won't that prevent the people inside from getting any air and therefore be in danger of suffocating?

Doggone it! Why do our people miss these things? But, say, I think I've got an answer to that. We should tell everyone to stock up on balloons. Then, if the warning system hits red, they can all blow into their balloons and keep them as an emergency air supply.

Mr. President, there are times when your lucidity, your clear thinking, leaves me simply flabbergasted.

Gee, thanks, mighty nice of you to say so. If I'm known for anything, it's for my clear thinking.

Something I find puzzling is why on one of the U.S. lists of weapons of mass destruction there is mention of the thyroid gland.

And you don't know what it is?

Oh, yes, Sir, I do indeed know what it is. But I do not understand why it should be mentioned together with hazardous devices, radiation threat, dirty bombs, and so on.

Well, our boys probably know something you don't. Let me assure you that if anyone tries to attack us with those glands, we'll be ready and I'm sure we've got the capability to destroy every last one of them.

That, if I may say so, is a very sobering thought.

I'm glad to hear you say that. Ever since I was born again sober thoughts are the only ones I have. What I can't understand is why some people are so critical of our homeland security measures.

Well, Sir, I believe they think the measures being taken are somewhat excessive and could lead easily to abuse. You know, putting so many agencies under one roof, such as the Border Patrol, Customs Service etc. They don't see too much danger of terrorism from Mexicans crossing the border to work as cooks and gardeners in Los Angeles or as cardiologists in Rochester and Houston. Or indeed from Canadians who all seem eager to get onto American TV to tell jokes. Maybe we should keep in mind what someone famous once said on this very subject – the plea for security could well become a cloak for errors, misjudgements and other failings of government.

Sure as heck whoever said that was some bleedin' heart liberal.

The man who said it has been called many things but never that. Actually, Sir, it was said during President Eisenhower's Administration by Mr. Richard Milhous Nixon who was then vice-president.

11. The Rocky Road to Nowhere

Good morning, Mr. President.

Good morning, good to see you again. Things seem to be going pretty well in Iraq, don't they?

Well, Sir, I looked at the latest news this morning and I see you are so pleased with how things are progressing there that you are now preparing, or indeed have already prepared, a road map for the Middle East.

What channel did you see that on?

I don't usually look at news on the TV any more. I find I get a greater variety of opinions on the Internet.

Don't mention that word to me. I'm told a lot of very nasty things are said about me on that thing. And it's all Al Gore's fault.

I'm sorry, Mr. President, I don't understand. Why is anything said on the Internet Mr. Gore's fault?

Well, didn't he invent it? That and the web thing. And all those lies about what he calls his Information Highway that he is always gabbing about.

I must confess I never knew Mr. Gore invented the net and the web, or that the information highway was his. And I have to say he always struck me as being a very truthful person.

I can tell you that the highway along which he says he and millions of others have travelled — that's a laugh — doesn't exist.

You astonish me, Sir. My impression was of a super highway with a very heavy load of traffic.

That's what he'd like you to think. Look, every time I'm in the car going anywhere at all I keep a close lookout on the road signs and never once did I see anything pointing to any information highway.

Well, Sir, as you never travel alone maybe your companions distract you with their chatter so you cannot keep as keen a lookout as you might wish.

Yeah, I thought of that so I asked my driver to find out where it went and let me know.

And what did he tell you.

It's the darndest thing. He's a very responsible guy so when he didn't report for work the next day we were real concerned. His wife said he'd left home as usual but he never showed up.

That must have been quite alarming. You did not think he could have been kidnapped?

That was the first thing we thought. We sent some agents to search for him and they found him miles away from the White House, in a side street, doing some kind of dance — they said it looked like a Highland fling — and singin' "You'll take the high road and I'll take the low road". One of the agents said it was subreal.

Sur.

Yes?

It's sur.

I know it's Sir. You've got to call me that 'cos I'm the President.

Thank you, Mr. President, Sir, for clearing that up. But about your driver, I can well understand your concern. What did you do?

We had to get a shrink to look at him. After all, we can't have mentally unbalanced people riding in the President's car, now can we?

Definitely not, Sir, that would be too many, I mean too much. But was the psychiatrist able to throw any light on the matter?

I got my people to bring him into the White House. It was bad luck that as soon as I asked him what the driver's symptoms meant, he had some kind of attack. Before he could answer he started shaking all over and he pulled out a Kleenex and was blowing his nose like mad. He couldn't stop long enough to answer me. I can tell you we had to get him out of there mighty quick. I couldn't risk catching any virus from him, especially that Russian one. It wouldn't surprise me if that guy Putin had a hand in that.

What Russian one, Sir? Oh, I see, you mean the SARS virus? I shouldn't worry; I strongly suspect that, even if the psychiatrist's condition proves to be SARS, it is a totally innocuous strain. But I'm really sorry to hear the information highway doesn't exist. I was hoping it might somehow be connected to the road in the Middle East for which you are preparing your map.

Oh, shucks. Everyone keeps asking me about that. Don't people realize there's no road, so it's not the kind of map you can buy in a store. It's in my head. What you would call a fig leaf.

Would I, Sir?

Sure, you remember when you said the president you were talking about was a fig leaf for your imagination? It's like that.

Oh, I see, when I mentioned he was a figment of my imagination. I believe a lot of people have already grasped that about your roadmap. So, as you say the highway does not exist and neither does the road, we could say it's a case of never the twain shall meet.

You know, you have an annoying habit of going off on a tangle. We were talking about highways and roads and suddenly you bring a train into it. Anyhow, trains don't meet anyone. People meet trains. By the way, I never noticed your speech impediment before.

It's only noticeable when I am confused. And I apologize for going off on a tangent. Thinking about the Middle East reminded me of a book about the Orient Express. That's a......

Yeah, yeah, I know what it is. They kill people on it. I saw the movie.

So what you have devised might be called a virtual road map for a virtual road along which as many can travel as take the non-existent highway. And, of course, being virtual it has no beginning and no end and can lead to anywhere and to nowhere. A very interesting concept.

There you are! Now, I ask you, nobody could object to a virtuous road map for the Middle East, could they? And I thought it up all by myself, although I've heard Donald Rumsfeld is trying to take the credit, as he often does.

I do not believe you should be concerned about that, Sir. Everyone knows you thought it up. And, as it's a road without milestones, a great advantage is, should that awkward question crop up about "how many miles to Babylon?" you can give any answer you like and no-one can contradict you.

12. Oh, What a Tangled Web

Good morning, Mr. President.

Good morning. It's a long time since I've seen you. I've missed our little chats. I heard you've been in England and other places over there.

Yes indeed, Sir. I spent some time getting up to date on events in Mr. Blair's country. And in Europe too. I saw your Mission Accomplished photo on the Abraham Lincoln a few months ago. If I may say so, you looked very macho, the very picture of a Commander-in-Chief.

I did, didn't I? I don't understand why so many complained about it. A Commander-in-Chief isn't supposed to look like a wimp. I guess some people will complain about anything. But now that you mention Tony, I'm sure glad he's finally shut up.

Shut up, Sir? I thought you liked hearing him agreeing with everything you said.

That's all very well. But he was shooting his mouth off and waving bits of paper about in the House of Commons with intelligence information on Saddam Hussein's weapons of mass destruction. Rumsfeld and, I'm sorry to say, me too, passed it on to the people as gospel. Then we find out that the Brits got it from our own intelligence people who happened to be wrong because they were quoting their intelligence people who got it from the Italian intelligence people who got it from someone who gave them a forged document. And they say some guy on the Internet comes into it somewhere, so it wouldn't surprise me if Al Gore had a hand in it.

People in Britain too are worried about the intelligence reports they are getting. And many, especially of the older generations, are not at all happy to see a British Prime Minister waving a bit of paper about. It reminds them of an earlier Prime Minister, Neville Chamberlain, who did the same thing. It gives them a kind of frisson.

I'm sure sorry to hear that but no doubt there's something they can take for it. What do you make of Tony's mouthpiece? The one I saw on TV. As far as I can see, he doesn't know what's going on in his office, didn't do anything himself but says mistakes were made although nobody made them. Still, they say he's a smart guy.

Sir, I can say that Alastair Campbell, the Prime Minister's Director of Communications and Strategy, is known to be an excellent fisherman. Very good at producing red herrings although, now that he's on his way out, many people think that one of his red herrings may have turned out to be a piranha.

Well, all I can say is that Tony's attempts to help me caused me a heck of a lot of trouble. Everything was going along great until he spouted about his dossier and now everyone here wants to know what hand we had in, what do they say, sexing it up? I don't get that. First of all, why can't they call it a file instead of that foreign name, and I don't see what sex has to do with a file. But then, as I think you know, I've been leading a quiet life since I was born again, so I'm not up to speed about what's going on in that direction. What would you have called it?

It is an odd expression, Sir, and it was a mistake to use it. I believe if the word sex had not been used there would not have been all the fuss.

You mean the Brits don't like sex?

Oh yes, Sir, they like it all right. It's just that they don't like talking about it. If I had to describe it I would have said they had tarted it up.

Yeah, that sounds just great. It gives it a nice homey, apple pie-ish feeling. But if he wanted to talk about Saddam Hussein's weapons why didn't he mention that trailer they found with all that stuff to make biological weapons?

Actually, Sir, what they found was that the trailer was meant to make hydrogen for weather balloons.

That sounds like a real tall tale to me. Where did you get that from?

From a report one of your own Defence Intelligence Agency's engineering experts wrote in May.

Is that a fact? It just goes to show, as I think I said before, that guy will stop at nothing. Now he's going after our weather. The next time I talk to the country I must remember to mention the weather terrorists. Do you think he had anything to do with that terrible hurricane Fabian? It's a good thing Bermuda got in the way and stopped it from reaching us. Who's the head of government there? I like to call and say thanks.

Bermuda is still British, Sir, so although Mr. Blair is not their prime minister he might be a good person to contact, unless you want to go straight to the Queen as head of state.

No, I believe I'll stick to Tony. I haven't seen him for some time so I'm glad I can thank him for something. He must think I've been giving him the cold shoulder. I sure miss those jars of Marmite. But there's something I don't get that everyone was talking about. I threw out a few suggestions but nobody gave me any feedback.

What would that be, Mr. President. As you know, I shall do my very best to clear up any doubts you might have. If I am able to that is.

It's this business about those guys in Iraq trying to have cake sent from Africa. I don't get it. Why go all the way there? Don't they have any cake shops in their own country? And they say it was yellow cake. You know Laura makes a pretty neat lemon sponge cake. Maybe after we have made friends with the people there it would be a nice gesture for me to send one to the head of their government, when we appoint him that is. As a kind of peace offering. How does that hit you?

The cake? Oh, I see, you mean the idea. I believe the yellow cake they are talking about has other, somewhat more explosive ingredients, even more explosive than the British bangers. But it is certainly worth a try. Maybe when they get it we will finally see the dancing in the streets.

I'll get my guys on to it. Well, I've gotta go. When we next get together I'll like to talk about the Italian guy, the one who's just been to see me.

Mr. Berlusconi. I look forward to that.

13. O Sole Mio

Good morning, Mr. President.

Oh, hi. Nice to see you again so soon. Now, tell me about this Berlusconi, Benito is it? He's just been over here. Laura served spaghetti and meat balls for dinner to make him feel at home. He seems very friendly to us and supports our stand on Iraq.

Sir, I am afraid you have the name wrong. Benito was another Italian, before your time, although his name keeps cropping up, actually in connection with Mr. Berlusconi whose first name is Silvio.

No, I don't think that can be right because that's the stuff Laura uses to polish the flatware.

Oh, I assure you it is right, Sir, only Silvio has two 'i's'.

Well I know he has. I told you, I've just seen him. I'm sure I'd have noticed if he only had one. Besides, it would have been on the Health Channel's medical mysteries. Didn't he make some fuss and tell a German guy he should be in a play about the Nazis?

Yes, he did, Sir. He said the German representative to the European Union could take the part of a Kapo, or a Nazi concentration camp guard. People were quite taken aback because, you see, he is the heir to the Benito you mentioned who was the Duce, or what in Texas you would call the head honcho, of the Fascists and who was a great friend of Hitler and his Nazis. The Fascist party was completely totalitarian and controlled the press, radio and other media; there was no television in those days. He also made laws just to suit himself.

And, of course Berlusconi would have none of that so he doesn't want to be associated with this Benito guy.

That's the odd thing, Sir. He, Mr. Berlusconi, owns most of the Italian press and television and other media and makes laws for his own purposes.

Can he do that? Maybe I should tell Dick to get in touch with him for a few tips.

Dick? You mean Mr. Cheney, the Vice President. Does he want to make laws to suit himself?

He sure does. Too many lawmakers are asking too many questions about his finances. A law to shut them up would be a great help. So this guy Berlusconi said the wrong thing?

Well, Sir, people think he should really keep quiet about the Nazis because unkind comparisons might be made, indeed I believe are already being made. His use of the word Kapo, spelt with a "k", was unfortunate because they have the same word in Italian, only spelt with a "c", and it means the head man in a Mafia family and a word frequently mentioned in the same sentence as Mr. Berlusconi's name.

But he got elected didn't he. And I think he expects to get in again. What's your take on that?

I really couldn't say, Sir. He is not as popular as he was. His countrymen are getting a bit tired of hearing their prime minister called a clown, or worse, by other members of the European Community. So he might be looking for another job one of these days.

You say he has a lot of media experience. Maybe he could try his hand at the movies or television. Movie stars become politicians so why shouldn't a politician become an actor? Senator Fred Thomson did and they say he's just as good an actor as he was a senator. By the way I'm expecting another call from Arnie any day now, so I could ask him if he could help out.

You mean Mr. Schwarzenneger? I understand he wants to be governor of California.

He sure does. And it wouldn't surprise me if he had his eyes set on even becoming president one day.

Correct me if I'm wrong, but I don't think anyone not born in the United States can become president.

I don't know about that, I've never had to think of it. But he has a great handicap that might make people not want to vote for him.

You mean they might not like to vote for a former muscle-man-of-the-year, or someone who has made so many disparaging remarks about women and immigrants, of whom he is one?

Oh, no, that's not what I meant. It's his accent. The people might not want a president they couldn't understand.

I believe they're used to it.

What's that?

I said, I believe they'd get used to it.

Yeah, I guess so. You know, I've gotta see an ear doctor. My hearing doesn't seem to be as sharp as it used to be. But getting back to Berlusconi. The last time I spoke to Arnie he told me the producers of the Sopranos are having a problem with the guy who plays Tony, the star. Suppose I suggest they try to get Berlusconi to take over, as he knows so much about TV. Do you think he'd be interested? But maybe he couldn't do it if he's no acting experience.

Well, Sir, he has the name and he has the looks for the part, and I have no doubt he also has the right contacts to coach him. And he's quite well known for his histrionics. Besides, as he is Italian his pronunciation of "capish" is excellent which, as you know, is a sine qua non for any actor in a movie about the mob.

I never knew that. Well then, if he's got that cine thing he might as well use it. I just thought of something. Don't you think it's a coincidence that the three of us, Bush, Blair and Berlusconi, who agree on everything, have the same initial? Almost like fate. Maybe we could call ourselves the Bee-Bees. What do you think?

I don't think that is at all a bad idea, Sir. After all, Mr. Berlusconi used to be a cruise ship singer and it is said he was much in demand as a dancing partner for lonely ladies. If you do decide to form a group, he could probably be the lead singer and give you a few tips.

Tony's conversation with Cherie

Tony, you're looking quite cheerful today.

I've just had a call from George.

George who?

Bush, of course, who do you think?

Oh, that's a surprise. I thought you weren't on speaking terms.

Of course we are. Although it's true he's been a bit peeved ever since he made that statement using our dossier as his source. But it wasn't my fault. I didn't know it wasn't absolutely one hundred per cent true.

Oh, I believe you. After all, everyone says you're sincere. But I have an inkling that some people might wonder which is more alarming, a prime minister who lies through his teeth, or one who stands up in Parliament, says what he sincerely believes and then confesses he had no idea what he was talking about. What do you think?

Honestly, Cherie, sometimes I can't help wondering if...... oh, never mind. As I was saying before I was interrupted, George called and this time I believe he really is as bonkers as we thought.

So what did he have to say now?

He started off by saying he had a lot to tell me to bring me up to speed. First of all he thanked me for keeping Fabian away from the United States. I thought he meant the Fabian Society because of what he would call its left wing tendencies. You know they have been making some harsh comments about free trade and globalization.

I hope he doesn't find out you gave their annual lecture in July or he might go off in a huff again. Didn't we hear something about Fabian on the telly? To do with the Atlantic, I think.

I have no idea what he meant. Anyway, he made no more sense when he went on to talk about Saddam Hussein's weather terrorists and what steps his guys were planning to intercept them.

It's a good thing he didn't think that one up before you prepared your dossier or that might have ended up in it too. Well, if it's a case of thwarting weather terrorists that's probably where you can offer him expert help.

How on earth can I do that?

By sending him some of our weather forecasters. Even with satellites they still manage to get it wrong, so they would thoroughly confuse any terrorists trying to attack the weather. Still, I must admit they're a bit better than they were. At least they no longer forecast rain with occasional showers or sunny with bright intervals, as they used to do.

Oh, really, Cherie, you do exaggerate! Although I do remember forecasts of heavy fog with limited visibility. I wonder if we still have stocks of those old World War Two barrage balloons or what the Americans call blimps? They could float over their main cities to deflect anti-weather weapons launched by the weather terrorists. If we have, I'll offer them to him when I call him back.

I wish you wouldn't, call him back I mean but, if you must, you better make sure that after all these years the barrage balloons are still in good shape. It would be humiliating if they didn't blow up properly or sagged and floated down onto Times Square. But is that all he had to say?

No, he then started talking about Bermuda. Said he'd always wanted to visit it as he knew there was no greater example of Western civilization. No-one admires Bermuda more than I do. I always enjoy my holidays there but I'd hardly place it together with Greece or Rome.

Have you forgotten the Triangle? No doubt George thinks that's a mathematical discovery beyond anything the Arabs came up with. And then there are the shorts which he probably considers to be one of the 20th century's greatest inventions.

You're probably right. He then changed the subject completely and said he is very concerned about Iraq, which is no surprise. Strange, though, that his main worry seems to be the pastry shortage.

Pastry? Well, there must be a shortage since there's a shortage of everything else, water, power, even petrol although the Americans and others too I might add, thought they'd be swimming in it. But I wouldn't call it odd, I'd call it bizarre.

Could it be another sign of his obsession with food? First it was eggs, then barbecues, the Kennedys not giving their guests enough to eat and once, when I mentioned José Aznar, out of nowhere he started extolling the virtues of parsley. I think it all began with the French fries and the French toast. Now it seems he's thinking about sending in some people to get the pastry shops back in business, in Baghdad to begin with, and it seems he wants to get Laura involved.

What, you mean a Pastry Patrol? But why Laura?

He says no-one knows how to make better...., oh, what was it? Oh, yes, lemon meringue pies, and he wants to send them to Iraq. You know, I've heard of people having a foot fetish but never a food fetish. Do you think that's possible?

Why not? I'm told that when alcoholics like your old friend are forced off the booze they often turn to other compulsions. But if the pies are anything like the cherry pie you described, wouldn't sending them come under the heading of cruel and unusual punishment? Was that all he said?

No, but the rest was even more incoherent. That we Brits, as he insists on calling us, should really try to get over our hang up about sex. It was perfectly all right, he said, to mention it, or even to write about it, as long as we didn't actually do anything about it.

You misheard. He must have said Sekt, the German bubbly. As the Germans are still not being as helpful as he hoped, he probably wants it banned.

I tell you it was sex he was talking about and it's not the first time. You remember I told you about that ghastly barbecue when he talked about mixed company and said he understood all about urges? He can't seem to get his mind off it. Could it be another fetish like his food fetish? Can people have more than one at a time? The mind boggles.

I hardly dare ask if there's anything else.

I'm afraid there is. He started talking about Berlusconi who had just been to see him. He had it on very good authority that he might lose his job, although he didn't mention that to Silvio so as not to upset him. And that he might be interested in American TV. That's the first I've heard of Berlusconi wanting to buy U.S. television stations. He'd probably have to become a U.S. citizen to do that, wouldn't he?

Yes, I suppose he would. But the Australian Rupert Murdoch did it, so why not your Italian pal Silvio. Although it is rumoured that Murdoch, desperate as he is to get into the Chinese market, is often seen shuffling in and out of the Chinese Consulate, probably trying to become Chinese.

I don't know why you call Berlusconi my pal. But to get back to George. When he finished talking about Berlusconi he said something about his horses, which I didn't get.

Are you sure? What exactly did he say.

I can't remember but it was something about gee-gees. Imagine! At his age.

Oh, I don't know, didn't you tell me he once talked about his daddy. If he says that, then there's nothing odd about calling his horses gee-gees. I expect it was something about his ranch.

Only called did he call George Senior his daddy. He usually calls him dad and he does that because his Father is the One

Above. He said nothing about any ranch. But you're not going to believe what comes next.

Tony, why is it that whenever you talk about your conversations with George you sound just like Ripley?

As I was saying, the odd thing is, straight from talking about the gee-gees, I mean horses, he seemed to be asking me if I'd like to join a choir. What do you make of that?

What I make of it, my dear Tony, is that he obviously never heard you warbling in the shower, even if you both do use the same toothpaste.

I'll ignore that remark. I suppose I'll have to call him back but I'm dreading it. Oh, by the way, remind me to get on to Jack Straw first thing tomorrow. It's a bit late now.

The Foreign Secretary. Why, you and George aren't planning another war? Against France, perhaps?

Don't be absurd. I want him to put a few jars of Marmite in the Washington diplomatic bag for George.

14. A Fishy Tale

Good morning, Mr. President.

Hi, you've been away again. But so have I. I was in New York you know.

Yes, Sir, I had heard. In fact, I saw your address to the United Nations on television. I hope you enjoyed your visit to New York.

There's no way I can enjoy a visit there. It always seems like foreign territory to me. If my people hadn't fixed a meeting for me with a group of CEOs it would have been a total disaster. Especially that U.N. thing.

Yes, that must have been difficult. The delegates did not appear to be persuaded by your plea for help to get you out ..... I mean to help you out with Iraq.

What really bugged me was Kofi Annan insulting the coalition like that and his nasty dig at Tony.

I think that's something I must have missed. I find it hard to credit that Mr. Annan would insult anyone, certainly not in public. Of course, what he may say in private is something else. If I may ask, Sir, how exactly did he insult the coalition?

Didn't you hear him call it a haddock coalition? That was a pretty snide reference to Tony's habit of always ordering fish and chips. By the way, you know, we can get pretty good fish and chips in Washington. He once invited me and I recall he did indeed ask for haddock. As they had no catfish, I had cod.

You and Mr. Blair went to a fish and chips shop in Washington?

No, of course not, we ordered to go.

Well, Sir, I did not hear Mr. Annan make any reference to fish in his remarks. He did call it an <u>ad hoc</u> coalition – without an initial "h".

There you are! He was obviously mocking the way the Brits talk. I've heard them on the BBC.

It's true some Londoners are parsimonious when it comes to using the initial letter "h", but I believe Mr. Annan was referring to the coalition being put together rather hastily and to its composition: countries like Albania, Azerbajan, Micronesia, the

Marshall Islands and other coalition members that hardly have the resources to contribute much in the way of troops for Iraq or in helping to finance the country's reconstruction. Mr. Annan's reference may very well have been to the coalition's incongruity rather than any ichthyoidal feature.

I never said it was whatever you called it. We call it a coalition of the willing (Tony helped me think that one up), which means friendly countries determined to help us impose the American way of life on the people of Iraq, whether they like it or not. Who can see anything wrong with that?

I don't think you need worry, Sir. I can assure you most people outside the U.S.A. have grasped what your coalition is all about.

I'm sure glad to hear it. There suddenly seem to be an awful lot of Doubting Thomas's around. But let's talk about something more cheerful. How about that Arnie? Ain't it somethin' that an Austrian immigrant can become governor of a state, and California at that? As they say, only in America.

Actually, Sir, there is a precedent in Mr. Schwarzenegger's own country. Some years ago a fellow countryman of his emigrated to Germany, became its leader – or fuehrer as he was called – took total control and then invaded and conquered many surrounding countries.

I wonder if Arnie knows about that?

Yes, he does indeed. Reliable sources have reported he has expressed his admiration for some of that leader's qualities, especially his determination, ability to communicate and his rise from rags to riches, or poor-boy-makes-good success.

Well, you've to admit Arnie knows how to persuade people. He got the votes in spite of all that talk about how he groups women. I wonder how he does that. Do you think he separates them according to age, or size?

I believe his specialty is groping rather than grouping and size, shape or age does not matter. As to his ability to persuade, that is probably inherited. It's a talent people have where he comes from. The leader I mentioned even invaded Austria, his own country, and when he sent his troops in, people really did dance in the streets. But then, when he eventually fell, the very same people managed to convince the rest of the world that they were his victims. A truly amazing PR exercise.

Wow! Maybe I should tell Rummy to ask him for a tip or two.

Mr. Rumsfeld? Yes, I've heard he could do with a few lessons on how to communicate. If they got together, maybe with Mr. Kissinger as mentor, they could all chat in their native language.

I'll put the idea to Arnie and see how it strikes him. But perhaps first of all I should run it by Condi. I'll bring it up when we have our next workout.

You work out with Miss Rice, Sir?

I sure do. That's when she gives me her input on events and people, especially Don as she always seems to have a lot to say about him. She tells me how things are unfolding and so on.

She no doubt briefs you about their strategy meetings.

Gosh, I don't know about that. I must confess I often lose track of what she says. She does drone on, so I tend to switch off and just say yeah, okay, or sure why not, from time to time.

But, Sir, might not that be somewhat dangerous?

It sure might. The day after one of our workouts I was told the New York Times *(I never read it) said I had appointed her head of the Iraq Strategy Group she dreamed up. I can tell you Rumsfeld was hopping mad and didn't hesitate to let everyone know about it.*

Yes, I had heard the sparks really flew.

They flew all right. That's one troubled fire I had to pour a lot of oil on.

With quite incendiary results I should imagine.

I don't know what you'd call them. All I know is he stopped babbling, but not before he claimed it was his idea. Maybe the Group can think up a strategy to deal with that Iraqi scientist who had all that poison in his refrigerator. Botu something or other. I guess he was planning to spread it all over Iraq, or even send it here.

The botulinum toxin? There are different opinions about his intentions. I have it on very good authority that a list of names was found beside the vial, said to be the scientist's targets, some of them in the United States. It seems he was hoping to make a killing.

Gee, they never said anything to me about that. Any idea who they were? Have they been told?

Yes, apparently they have.

Well, it's a good thing he was stopped before he could assassinate anyone.

Oh, I'm sorry, Sir. I didn't make myself clear. When I said killing I was talking about the stock market. His plan seems to have been to convert his botulinum into a material that would make a better product than Botox which, as you know, is used to eliminate wrinkles. He claims his product is superior because it can be rubbed onto the skin as a cream instead of injected. Apparently American magazines have found their way onto the Iraqi market and the local ladies are clamouring for all kinds of beauty products. He wanted to get in on the ground floor, sell his product to the highest bidder among the cosmetic companies on his list, buy up shares in the company and then unload them when the price shot up. So, as you can see, speed is of the essence.

He seems to have the right ideas. Maybe we could use him in some way. As an adviser to Halliburton perhaps?

Good thinking, Sir, although I have a suspicion that it will take more than a spot of botulinum to iron out the Halliburton wrinkles.

Tony's conversation with Cherie

Tony, what's up? Another chat with your pal George?

I called him back today. Do you want to hear about it or not?

Wild horses wouldn't make me miss it. What did he have to say this time?

First of all he said he was sorry I was not at the U.N. General Assembly.

A lot of people wondered why you didn't go to the meeting that was to defend your marching off to war, figuratively speaking of course, shoulder to shoulder, with George. The consensus was you were trying to distance yourself from him.

What nonsense! You know very well I had other very important things to do.

Yes, of course. What were they? Attending a school prize giving, polishing up your speech to the Labour Party Conference, tying your shoelaces?

Really, Cherie, this is no time for sarcasm. George then said something very strange.

You amaze me!

Yes, he said he had asked his people to send a strong note of protest to Kofi Annan about the haddock.

About the U.N. restaurant food? I'm sure the Secretary General has much more on his plate than haddock at the moment. Besides, I doubt George ever ate there. And shouldn't any complaints about the food be addressed to the chef?

I suppose they should. He went on to say that no nasty remarks about the coalition could be made if we British, or perhaps I should say Brits, would only learn to appreciate catfish.

What in heaven's name is that?

I hadn't a clue so I asked the Foreign Office to get on to our Consulate in Houston to find out. Apparently it's yet another Texan culinary delight.

Does it prowl or does it swim?

I never thought to ask, but he recommend-
ed we try the blue or the flathead. The
other varieties are not so tasty, he says.

Tony, I told you before, you ought to let me
listen in on the extension. I can't believe
he really says what you say he says.

You know I can't do that. It just wouldn't
be proper. But do you really think I could
make up any of this?

No, I suppose not. Your imagination
doesn't run to that. The look on your face
tells me there's more

He's worried that people don't take the
coalition of the willing seriously. As he
can't get France, Germany or Russia to
join, he wants to give it more prestige by
persuading some other European powers
to come on board and he asked me for
my take on Andorra and San Marino.

Well, there's no doubt it does not have the
same weight as the coalition of the unwill-
ing. But I'm surprised he even knew of the
existence of those countries.

Apparently one of his hobbies is sticking
pins in maps.

A pity one of his pins didn't hit the Vatican. The Swiss Guards would make a colourful addition to the occupying... I mean coalition forces.

He mentioned something about Arnold Schwarzenegger and his, that is George's, workouts with Condoleeza Rice or Condi as he calls her. I didn't quite get it, but I suppose Schwarzenegger would be the person to show them the best routines to follow. After all, he was muscle-man-of-the-year many times. He also told me about an Iraqi scientist who has discovered a new anti-wrinkle cream and he said he thought he'd do me a favour by passing along the tip.

Well, although it's true your put-on-a-happy-face expression has been conspicuous by its absence of late, I think it was very tactless of George to be quite so blunt. What did you say?

I didn't know what to say, especially when he told me if I didn't act soon it would be too late. I tell you I felt quite depressed.

I hardly think it's up to George to criticize anyone's appearance. Only this morning I was rummaging through the attic when I stumbled across that signed photo of his you had removed from your office. You know, the one of him astride the Abraham Lincoln aircraft carrier with his Mission Accomplished banner.

When I told them to get rid of it, I didn't think it would end up there. Still, the main thing is I don't have to look at it

That photo shows his brow with more furrows than a ploughed field.

Then it's obvious he doesn't have the gift, when he looks at himself in the mirror, of seeing himself as others see him.

That's hardly surprising. I have been told, on the very best authority, that as soon as it was announced his brother had fixed things so that he would be President, all the mirrors in the White House and at Camp David were replaced. They had already been changed at the ranch.

What do you mean replaced? With what? Antique mirrors?

Don't you remember how, as children, we used to laugh our heads off at fairs looking into the distorting mirrors. Well, these are similar, only with the opposite effect. They make you look much better.

What would be the opposite of to distort? To entort?

I believe enhance would be the proper word. So, when George stands in front of a mirror what he sees reflected is himself saving Private Ryan, as John Wayne winning the Burma or some other World War II Campaign, or as Gary Cooper in High Noon rather than what most people know what he really is.

You mean with Laura at his side as Grace Kelly?

I don't think the mirrors' enhancing abilities are quite that powerful. Or it may be that George simply wants to use you as his guinea pig before he tries the remedy himself.

Honestly, Cherie, I don't know where you find your best authorities. Anyway, I can't worry about it at the moment. I've got George's visit to cope with. Oh, damn! I suppose I'll have to put the photo back for that.

Yes, worry is the worst possible thing for wrinkles. And I can't think the coming visit will do anything to improve things in that direction.

I'm hoping he'll be given a warm welcome.

Well, Tony, I'm sure you need have no concerns on that account. I bet you a pound to a penny that George's visit will generate more heat among the British Public than any other state visit ever has.

15. Uneasy Lies the Head...

Good morning, Mr. President. I hope I'm not interrupting.

No, come on in. I'm a bit rushed, almost ready to set out for London.

Yes, you must be quite excited.

I sure am. Staying at Buckingham Palace with the Queen and Prince Philip, a state banquet in my honour. By the way, you know about these things so maybe you can help us out.

I'd be delighted to, although I have not had too much contact with royalty, I must confess. What is it you would like to know?

I was wondering if the Queen will be wearing one of her crowns. And, if so, do you think we should get hold of one of those little ones for Laura to wear? What do you call them?

I believe you mean a tiara.

Yeah, that's right. What do you think?

Well, Sir, I doubt that when her Majesty dresses to dine she dons a crown. Even if she did, I honestly would not advise that Mrs. Bush wear a tiara.

Why not? You think the Brits wouldn't approve, especially the press?

On the contrary, I'm sure the British press would be in seventh heaven if Mrs. Bush turned up in a tiara. But I am thinking of your own people. They might object that it was over the top.

Well, gee, where else would they expect it to be?

Yes, of course. That's the only place it could be.

Well, then, I guess I'll tell Laura to keep it plain and simple.

Just be her usual self, you mean? Yes, I definitely believe that would be best.

There's something else I want to ask you. I'm supposed to meet the new leader of the Conservatives. Michael Howard, isn't it? I hear he's been called a caballero, as we say in Texas. That is, those of us who speak Spanish.

Are you sure you are not thinking of the other Conservative, Mr. Portillo, who is also Michael and once thought of as a sure thing to lead the Tories? He is the son of Spaniards after all, while Michael Howard's background is Romanian.

No, it was definitely Howard. And I am sure I heard it said he is something of a knight. Isn't that so?

What they actually say is that there is something of the night about Mr. Howard. The word used does not start with a k.

I know caballero starts with a c. I told you I speak Spanish. I once gave a speech in San Antonio and when I finished everybody stood up and cheered.

If you will allow me to say so, Mr. President, I would expect no less.

Gee, thanks. You sure know how to make a guy feel good. But if Michael Howard is Romanian, how are we going to talk? Is that language anything like Spanish?

Yes, it has a lot of similarities, but I can assure you Mr. Howard speaks exceptionally good English. About your visit. It must have been quite a job getting everything organized to handle your very large entourage.

My very large what?

The many people, I believe 700 is the number mentioned, accompanying you. How can I put it? Your very large posse.

I have people to look after that. I was on the phone to Tony telling him all about our arrangements, but I don't think he was paying much attention. His mind seemed to be wandering.

That does surprise me. I can hardly imagine anything that would concentrate his mind more than hearing about your 250 armed agents, the 35-car convoy, a decoy car and so on. What makes you think he was distracted?

He suddenly said something about throwing rocks at birds. I was quite shocked, especially after he's been making such a fuss about fox hunting. Birds are just as much God's creatures as foxes are.

I think I can explain. When he heard about your arrangements and your request that Buckingham Palace be made bombproof and the London underground, or subway, closed during your stay, he must have exclaimed "Stone the crows!" It's an English phrase expressing utter incredulity. He was probably expecting something on a slightly more modest scale. What was his comment about the underground?

He said he'd be very happy to do it but that the Mayor, a guy called Livingstone, won't allow it. Don't you think a head of government should be able to tell a mayor what to do? I know I do.

Kenneth Livingstone, or Red Ken as he is known in some quarters, is not a man who takes kindly to being given orders by Mr. Blair.

Is he Scottish or Irish?

I really don't know, Sir, he was born in London although it is true Livingstone sounds quite Scottish. But what makes you think so?

He's called Red so he must have red hair.

I have a feeling the colour refers to something else. If he ever had red hair he no longer does.

That's too bad. I know of a pretty neat product called Touch-It-Up. I'd be glad to take him some if it would help. Do you think he'd like it?

I've no doubt he would be quite dumb-founded at such an offer.

Then I'll put it on my list of things to do in London. You know, I've been doing my bit to prepare the way for the visit. I gave an interview to a guy from the BBC and to The Daily Telegraph newspaper. Did you hear about that?

Indeed I did. Shortly after you spoke to *The Daily Telegraph* Lord Conrad Black, the proprietors' CEO resigned, and it seems the newspaper is to be put up for sale. But, personally, I do not believe for a moment, as some claim, it has anything at all to do with your interview.

I don't understand what all the fuss is about. After all, it's not the first state visit they've ever had. They must have a lot of practice.

Yes they certainly have but they have never had a state visit quite like this. Mr. Blair seems to be finding it hard to justify putting the whole of London's police out in force for this particular one. Still, one sector of the population is quite thrilled that the constabulary will be occupied on that specific duty so they can go about their business unhindered.

I'm glad to hear that. Tony said some people were worried because so many of our guys will be carrying guns. Don't all their police carry guns?

Actually no, Sir. Very few of them do, at least as yet. And, as you know, as your country is world champion when it comes to friendly fire fatalities, the people are rather concerned that your agents might be tempted to break their own record, especially as you have requested they be immune from prosecution should any unfortunate incident occur. But I am pleased to say that problem at least has been solved.

You mean the people understand that accidents can happen?

The problem, Sir, was solved by making sure no people get anywhere near you so that your sharpshooters will have no-one to aim at, thus avoiding any mortal mishaps.

Wow! They seem to have thought of every-thing. A shame about the people though. I've been looking at videos of the Queen to practice the same wave but I guess I can't use it if there's no-one to wave to.

I am sure your wave can be put to use on another occasion although, if you were seen to wave, would it not rather defeat the purpose of the decoy car?

Maybe I could wave when I go to Down-ing Street. I'm told there will be quite a crowd nearby but not too close. Do you think they will give me a good reception?

No doubt Mr. and Mrs. Blair will greet you with open arms. And I understand a lot of people are going to a great deal of trou-ble to give you the welcome you deserve. One group is even preparing a statue of you which they plan to place on a ped-estal.

In Downing Street or outside the Palace?

I have heard it will be in Trafalgar Square, you know where there is a column to Nelson, the great British naval hero.

I haven't had a sailor suit since I was a kid. But maybe I could let them have the flying suit I wore on the aircraft carrier, so they can put it on the statue.

Your "mission accomplished" suit?

Now you know we don't mention that any more.

I don't know about the suit. But I'm sure they would love to have the banner to proudly display once they have done everything they plan to do with your statue.

I'll see what I can do but I don't think the banner is still available.. Well, I best be off. When I'm back I'll tell you about my visit.

Thank you, Sir. You cannot imagine how I look forward to it.

Tony's conversation with Cherie

Another phone call, Tony?

God, how I dread them!

Your pal George again?

Yes, talking about his visit.

Well, what did he say?

He said he didn't know what to do about Laura's head.

Isn't it a bit late to try to do anything about it? But then she is probably at a loss as to what to do about his, as many others are. What were his actual words?

That he would tell her to forget about putting anything on it and just keep it as simple as possible.

Well, no great effort needed there.

Don't be so catty. I know you miss your pal Hillary, but not every wife of a head of government can be a brilliant lawyer like you two. He then said he heard Michael

Howard is a real gentleman but he's concerned about his language.

What? I wouldn't call him a gentleman after all the nasty things he's said about you. But I must admit I've never heard anyone claim that he uses bad language.

I find George's insistence on telling me what I should do quite irritating. He now says I should try to be kinder to the birds. Haven't I always been?

Yes, of course you have. I've never noticed that you treat women any differently from the way you treat men. It's true you were pretty harsh on Clare Short when she resigned as International Development Minister over the war. But that, after all, was in defence of George. On the other hand, you were criticized for being very soft on Children's Minister Margaret Hodge when she insisted that the man who had been abused as a child in a home under her care was "extremely disturbed" and, because of that, his complaints should not be taken seriously.

Some malicious types are saying I let her off because her husband was once your boss and she's a friend of mine.

What rot! As if anyone could ever persuade you to do anything the majority of
people thought was wrong just because of
your special relationship. I wonder where
on earth George gets his information. His
intelligence service I suppose. From all
accounts, it is about as competent as our
own.

*He wanted to know if I had arranged for
the underground to be closed during his
visit. I told him I tried but Ken Livingstone
would have none of it. He also said he's
sorry about* The Daily Telegraph.

You mean he regrets giving the interview?
I can't think why. After all, it's his kind of
newspaper. Although I didn't read it, I'm
sure no awkward questions were asked.
So why in the name of heaven should he
have anything to be sorry about?

*Who knows? I mentioned it to our press
boys and they said he tried to get*
The Telegraph *to publish some of Laura's
recipes but they refused.*

Ah well, that explains it. They're in enough
trouble already without giving their readers any reason to sue them. Anything
else?

Yes. He's very happy so many of London's inhabitants are delighted that the whole constabulary will be assigned to protecting him. He assured me that target practice was never part of his plans, that he'll be very glad to donate his suit and that he is looking forward to seeing the banner flying.

His must mean the Royal Standard. Did you explain to him that it signifies the Queen is in residence and is not being put up to denote his presence?

No I did not. By the way, he's planning to do something very odd.

Whatever could that be?

For reasons unknown, he's going to bring some hair enhancer for Ken Livingstone.

16. How Now Brown Cow

Good morning, Mr. President. I hope you enjoyed your visit to England.

I sure did. I especially enjoyed the banquet. You know, I had asked the Brits not to serve any wines or other alcoholic drinks in my presence and they agreed. They had plenty of bottles of grape juice and apple juice that everyone seemed to be enjoying a lot but I couldn't see the brand as the waiters kept napkins over the labels. I just had some Coke. The Queen and Prince Philip had mineral water.

Did they indeed? I imagine they had downed a generous amount of G&T before they entered the dining room.

What's that? I suppose it's one of those teas the Brits like so much. But I didn't know they drank it just before dinner.

Actually Sir, it's gin.... ger tea. A great favourite of many members of the Royal family. They drink it every chance they get.

Is it something that's good for you?

Well, Sir, it most definitely raises the Royal Family's spirits.

Maybe I could get our ambassador to have some sent to Texas. How about that?

I doubt that it would travel well. I think it would be like your own moonshine. which of course I know you never touch since your rebirth. As you may be aware, if imbibed in Mayfair, or in Manhattan for that matter, it would taste quite different from when gulped in Galveston.

In any case everything went very well, don't you think so? I gave the spontaneous speech that the guys in Washington kept making me practice, over and over again. It got good reviews in the press the next day.

The practice was obviously well worth it. I hear special admiration was expressed for your pronunciation of nuclear.

Yeah, at last I got it, didn't I? But it was a real sweat I can tell you. As I was saying, staying at the Palace was a great treat. It's full of butlers and footmen. By the way, what do footmen do? As far as I could see, they just stood there. They don't seem to use their feet as much as you'd expect from the name.

They now write for newspapers and publish books. The lucky ones may even end up as very highly paid confidential advisers to Prince Charles.

That's just great. It's sure nice that the household help can look forward to promotion.

Yes, indeed, Sir. As they say, there's always room at the top for them provided, of course, they are willing to undertake tasks of an esoteric nature not normally included in the description of a footman's duties.

What counts is that they're willing to advance. Ain't it a real shame they didn't fix the ropes on the statue properly so that it toppled over? But I can't explain the fire.

Yes it was a shame. You see, Sir, they had very little time to prepare it and moor the ropes properly. I think I can explain the fire. As it was a bit dirty, they tried to clean it with petrol, I mean gasoline, and unfortunately it blazed out of control.

Well, in spite of that, I can say I thoroughly enjoyed myself. Then there was the great trip to Tony's home town up north. We went to a local tavern, or pub as they call it, where we had fish and chips, Tony's favourite as I think you know. They also served us peas they named after me, in my honour.

Oh, really, Sir, I hadn't heard that. What were they called if I may ask?

Bushy peas.

Weren't they mushy?

Sure they were. They had to squash them so they wouldn't fall off the back of the fork, which is how they eat them over there, although I can't imagine why. Tony and Cherie drank lemonade and I had non-alcoholic beer.

Typical pub fare. As I understand there was a helicopter hovering during your stay, the pub was surrounded by agents and you met a select and very carefully chosen group of Mr. Blair's constituents, I've no doubt the locals will be talking about it for a long time to come.

It was just great except for one thing.

What was that, Sir? I'm sure Mr. Blair will be disappointed if something was not quite right.

It's the name. It's called the Cow Done In. Now I've got a cattle ranch and, just like everyone else, I know cows have got to be done in. Otherwise, how could we have our barbecues? But I think it's kinda cruel to announce it to the whole world.

In fact, Sir, the pub is called the Dun Cow Inn. Dun is brown.

I know done is brown but I don't like it. I prefer my steaks rare. Still, I think we can say my whole stay there was quite a triumph, wouldn't you agree?

Oh absolutely, Sir, I believe we could classify it, to use a phrase *The Financial Times* employed in another context, as a catastrophic success.

Wow! I never expected it to go off with such a bang.

Actually, Sir, I believe the success lies in the fact that it went off without a bang.

Tony's conversation with Cherie

So the circus has finally left town. What a relief!

Oh, blast! There's the phone. It must be George to talk about his visitation.

You're not telling me I was in a divine presence and never knew it?

Don't be so silly. That's what the Americans call a visit. Now, you'll have to leave the room for a while since you can't be privy to our secret conversations. I'll call you back in ten minutes.

How do you know you can get him to stop talking by then? Besides, since you tell me all about them, I don't see what difference it makes.

I'll think of something. That the house is on fire. Telling you is not at all the same as letting you eavesdrop. If he ever asks me whether you know what we talk about I can honestly say you never listen in.

………………..

All right, Cherie! You can come back now, I've finished talking to George.

He must have felt very pleased with himself.

Oh, he obviously did.

All right, so what had he to say?

Although he'd been warned that it does not travel well, he'd still like to try some of the Palace's ginger tea. Have you ever heard of it?

Maybe it's something a butler brewed and gave to him. Probably nicked from a present Prince Charles brought back from one of the tours to the East so we'd better not get involved.

He loved the banquet and said it was a nice touch to serve the guests fruit juice. I told you saying the claret and white Burgundy were grape and apple juice would work. If we hadn't done that there would have been a sudden epidemic of Asian flu or something equally disabling among those invited.

Whoever thought that one up should be given a medal.

He's over the moon because his speech went down well and the press reviews were favourable, which I think they were in fact.

That he was actually able to articulate a coherent, although no doubt well rehearsed, speech seems to have had a mesmerizing effect on the newspapers. But I thought *The Independent's* tone of utter disbelief was decidedly condescending. I am told there were heated arguments among the editors about the headline, some suggestions being quite unprintable.

You really shouldn't tell me that you've been told these things without saying you told you. Do you remember who it was?

Yes, you know, it was what's his name. It will come to me in a minute. But go on, tell me what more did he say.

That he is very glad to hear the Palace domestic staff have such great career opportunities. And, of course, he was ecstatic about his stopover in Sedgefield. Very flattered that they named a dish after him. I don't know what he's talking about. All we had were fish and chips and mushy peas.

So everything in the garden was lovely, according to him?

Not quite. Out of nowhere, he said he understood that cattle had to be slaughtered but he would advise us not to advertise it.

He can't be harping back to the foot-and-mouth outbreak. That was ages ago and, anyway, the whole point was to advertise it. If we hadn't killed off all the infected or likely to be infected animals and made it public, the Americans would have been the first to complain. So what the devil is he talking about?

I have no idea. But at least we can be thankful that it went off all right. He seemed thrilled to bits with what he got out of the visit.

And well he might be. And of course you got something out of it too.

Did I really? I must say I hadn't noticed.

Yes, haven't you seen the report from Scotland Yard? In London, street crime and muggings went up by 20% while you were paying homage to your chum, or should I say buddy?

17. A Mystery Solved

Good morning, Mr. President.

Oh, hi. How're you doin'?

I'm fine thank you, Sir. I expect you have now fully recovered from what must have been a strenuous trip.

You mean my visit to Iraq to take a hard look at the situation there?

Actually, Sir, I was thinking of your trip to England. I believe your trip to Baghdad was somewhat shorter. Two hours at the airport, was it not? Still, no doubt it enabled you to talk to a wide representation of the local population and get a really in-depth grasp of how things are progressing.

No, I didn't talk to or even see any Iraqis. I went there to serve turkey to our boys and tell them they're doin' a great job.

That was very thoughtful of you. Did Mrs. Bush cook the turkey?

Heck, no. I think our boys have suffered enough. Ha, ha. That's a joke by the way. Not to be repeated.

My lips are sealed. So now I expect you are taking things easy, just getting ready for Christmas?

You're darn right I am. I see that soon after I got back from London that French guy, Jacques Chirac, went there. Was that another state visit?

No, Sir, the state visit will come later, this was just a friendly get together with Mr. Blair, although they did give him a guard of honour.

I don't get it. I thought the Brits were mad as hell at the French, so why be so nice to the guy?

Well, Sir, it is a strange relationship with many ups and downs but, when all is said and done, they do speak the same language.

I thought the French spoke their own language.

I was speaking figuratively, Sir. What I meant was that they have a great deal in common and have had for a very long time, ever since the Norman Conquest in 1066. So when Mr. Chirac and Mr. Blair get together they have no problem understanding one another.

I've got to admit I've never had any problem understanding him whenever we've been together. You can't help admiring him for how well he speaks English.

I'm sure Mr. Blair would be very happy to hear that.

I meant Chirac. You know, ever since my visit to London I've been taking a great interest in what the Queen has been up to. Now that I feel we're kinda buddies. I see she went to Nigeria. How did that go?

Apparently very well. Her most important event was a meeting with a group of local soap opera stars. I have been given to understand her advice was sought because of her long experience of the genre.

What about the reporter who got a job at the Palace as a footman and then started spilling the beans about what the Queen

has for breakfast and so on? Did they ar-
rest him?

No, Sir, they did not. The Lord Chancellor
was consulted but he could find no reason
to charge the reporter with lèse majesté
for telling *The Daily Mirror* readers that Her
Majesty keeps her breakfast cereal in Tupperware dishes rather than Royal Doulton
chinaware as one might expect. But he
has been forbidden by court order from
divulging any more Palace secrets. So we
still do not know whether the royal breakfast cereal is followed by royal kippers,
and I expect now we never shall.

They sure as heck didn't serve us any meals
on Tupperware. They had some real ele-
gant plates and great flatware. But I think
what you told me can be of great help to
us. Laura was asking what we could give
Her Majesty for Christmas. I wonder what
kind of Tupperware she has. Maybe we
could get some in a different colour.

They brought out their best dishes for you
because you were company. As to the
colour of the Tupperware, I do not know
whether that detail was given. But the
makers say the models she has are from

the seventies, so I am sure something more modern would be most welcome.

Well, I guess that's the last time anything like that will happen. Now they'll be more careful about anyone they might take on as a footman.

No doubt. Still, there was another similar incident that they managed to hush up. I am one of the very few people who know about it as it was told to me in the strictest confidence by the reporter concerned, who happens to be a friend of mine. No newspaper can publish it because the consequences might be dire.

Well, gee, now you've got me real curious. So, what was it?

A reporter from *The Daily Mirror's* chief competitor, *The Morning Glare*, disguised as a housemaid, got a job at the Palace. He gave as references his favourite tandoori takeout and the local bookmaker. The Palace called them and were given the assurances required.

I don't get it. If he's a man he must have used a girl's name so the people who gave the references must have noticed the difference.

The newspaper chose that particular reporter because his name is Francis which, as you know, spelt with an "e" instead of an "i" is a girl's name. So when the Palace asked about someone called Frances those consulted assumed it was the young man they knew as Francis rather than the person who apparently was the young female presenting the references.

Why did they want a chambermaid to work there? To find out what kind of sheets the Queen's uses? If they'd asked me I could've told them, since I slept there.

Oh, no, Sir. It was not that at all. One great mystery that has plagued the British public throughout Her Majesty's reign concerns the royal headgear. They have always been dying to know where the Queen gets her hats.

She must have someone to make them for her. I suppose a hat maker, someone like a dressmaker. You keep up with these things, so you must have a name.

I know that for some years the name of Mr. Freddie Fox was given as the Queen's milliner. But I have been told that it was just a front. He lent his name for the honour of having the royal stamp of approval but, apparently, when it got back to him that he was being referred to as the Mad Hatter he decided it was not worth it and let it be known he would no longer be called the royal modiste.

Gee, that must have been a real blow to Her Majesty. Still, I guess there were plenty of others waiting to take his place.

If any other name has ever cropped up, I have never heard of it. But the reporter I mentioned was able to worm his/her way into the confidence of a Woman of the Bedchamber and got the scoop from her.

Well, I've heard they make good hats in Paris. I hope you're not gonna say the Queen buys French hats.

No danger of that, Sir. I am sure no French chapelier has ever produced anything similar to grace any French head. The truth is rather more startling, I'm afraid, but at least it cleared up something that has always puzzled me.

What was that?

Whenever I see the Queen in one of her heady concoctions, it always reminds me of the holidays I used to spend in Germany by the banks of the River Rhine. Now I know why. You see, Sir, the royal chapeaux are brought to Windsor by a representative, sworn to secrecy of course, of the Kaufhof Department Store in Düsseldorf.

Tony's conversation with Cherie

Tony, what's happened? It's a couple of weeks since you've had a call from George? You haven't done anything to offend him I hope. You need all the friends you can get.

Of course not, though it seems he was a bit put out because we greeted Jacques Chirac with a guard of honour. He talked about his visit to Baghdad and how he served turkey to the troops. The bird they gave him was so tough he couldn't cut it.

You're not going to tell me they got Laura to cook it.

No, but she might as well have. Apparently it was one of those meant to be looked at and photographed but not eaten. By the way, he said the Queen should not have gone to so much trouble over the banquet and that they would have been quite happy to eat what the family eats.

A royal banquet with fish fingers or sausage and mash would have been a first.

He went on to mention something about a hatter in the spotlight. I asked him what he meant but he wouldn't say anything more because, he said, he was sworn to secrecy.

Oh, Lord, you don't think talk of a hatter means he's planning to give you one of those ten gallons or whatever they call them, do you?

God, I hope not! It was bad enough when I had to stomp around in those boots. My feet have never recovered. He also said there are great outlets in Virginia near Washington, much better than anything they have in Germany, and that I should tell our Ambassador so that he can give Her Majesty the tip.

By outlets I suppose he means markets, but for what? Horses perhaps? Given her Majesty's interest. But why Germany? I've never heard she went there for animals to improve her stable.

Don't forget the Royal Family has a long tradition of looking for breeding stock in that country.

Yes, but not of the four-legged kind and they had to stop doing it when they dropped the Saxe-Coburg-Gotha and Wurttenburg, not to mention the Schleswig-Holstein-Sonderburg-Glucksburg, and became the Windsors. Although there was a bit of a slip up with Philip when, besides all the above, he added Battenberg to the mix.

No, but it may have had something to do with that scandalous newspaper article because he said he heard Tupperware was again all the rage in England. I wish they had gagged that reporter before he mentioned it instead of afterwards. Now I suppose when Prince Charles goes off on one of his trips, instead of coming back with gold elephants, exotic jewels and other priceless gifts he'll be hauling back crates of plastic.

Well, at least that will make it less profitable for the Palace fences to flog the presents to the highest bidder.

18. Let Us Give Honours Where Honours Are Due

Good morning, Mr. President. Happy New Year.

Good morning. Same to you. Nice to see you again.

Thank you Sir. You must be delighted that Saddam Hussein has been captured.

You can say that again. Things couldn't be better. All those people who were afraid to cheer while he was free will now be out on the streets waving the Stars and Stripes.

And of course the oil can start to flow again.

Yeah sure, that too. But what I want to ask you about today is this honours business in England. Our Ambassador has just told me about it. I don't understand why so many titles and decorations are handed out to so many people. I guess they're the ones who've done somethin' real exceptional, but who decides who gets them?

There are a number of sub-committees, nine I believe. They get together and draw up a list of names to be presented to the Prime Minister who then passes them on to Her Majesty for the appropriate honour to be awarded.

What kind of awards are they?

Those most often awarded, in descending order of importance, are KBE's, the most sought after because the recipients have the right to put "Sir" before their names so that the whole world knows they've been honoured; then come the CBE's, the OBE's, and the MBEs. There are others, even more prestigious than the KBE's, but they are awarded to far fewer people.

What do the initials mean?

Knight Commander of the Order of the British Empire; Commander of the Order of the British Empire; Officer of the Order of the British Empire; and Member of the Order of the British Empire.

I thought there was no British Empire any more so how can it give out honours if it doesn't exist? Haven't all the colonies disappeared?

Indeed they have not, Sir. Her Majesty still reigns over her Dominions in, let me see, oh yes, Pitcairn Island, the Sandwich Islands, St. Helena, Montserrat and, of course, we must not forget Gibraltar and the Falkland Islands.

But don't Spain and Argentina claim the last two?

Yes they do, but so far Britain has managed to hang on to them. As to why honours are awarded in the name of a non-existent Empire, I believe there are many people in Britain, especially on the nominating sub-committees, who have not yet noticed that it has vanished. In any case, I think you will agree it sounds better to give someone the title of Knight Commander of the Order of the British Empire rather than making him a Knight Commander of the Order of the Sandwich.

Who are the people who get knighthoods? They must have discovered cures for life-threatening diseases or something like that.

One of the recent recipients of a KBE is Mr. Clive Woodward, which now makes him Sir Clive. He is the coach of the English rugby team that beat Australia in

November to win the World Rugby Cup. The team captain got a CBE, the best player an OBE and the rest of the team were given MBE's. It usually takes much longer for awards to be handed out but it was such an amazing achievement that the nominating sub-committees made a special effort to put them on a fast track so they could be included in the New Year's Honours List. After all, to get to the final the team had to outdo such rugby powers as Tonga, Samoa and Fiji.

Wow, they must have really whacked the Aussies. What was the score? I guess it makes the recent 38-7 win by the New England Patriots over the Buffalo Bills look pretty weak.

Actually, Sir, they beat them by one dropped goal which, although I know very little of American football, I think must be something like a touchdown. As it happened in the last seconds of extra time it could have gone either way. But it was exceptional because, if I am not mistaken, the last time England won a world title for any kind of football was in 1966. So, as you will no doubt understand, when the team got back home they were given a huge parade and generally treated as heroes, especially by the younger generations for whom it was a first taste of national football glory.

Did any other sports figures get awards?

Oh, yes, one of the most popular was tennis star Tim Henman, who became an Officer of the Order of the British Empire and whose citation, which mentioned him as being "one of the best players Britain has produced for years", was widely applauded.

He must have won lots of those English tennis tournaments, at Wimbledon I think it is, to deserve that.

In fact, Sir, he has never won a Wimbledon title; the last native son to do that was Fred Perry in 1936, but Mr. Henman is recognised as being very good at getting the ball over the net. And then, of course, you have the awards given to stars from the entertainment industry, making some people believe that the Empire refers to the many Empire Theatres that used to exist in Britain and of which there are still a few left.

Don't any women get awards?

Yes, indeed they do get awards but not nearly as many as men get. The Honours list also includes a few of what are now known as ethnic minorities. Still, the smaller numbers of both these groups can be explained when we remember that the sub-committees' members are overwhelmingly white male civil servants over 50, which no doubt explains why one out of every 123 civil servants leaves the Service clutching a gong. The highest honour a woman can receive is to be made a Dame.

Gee, I don't think an honour like that would go down too well among our American gals. But it's a shame we don't have something like an honours list here. I'd love to be able to hand out, what is it you call them? Pongs?

Gongs, Sir. Still, when the list of names is published, some people think your word might better describe it. But I believe the United States has a somewhat similar system, your Congressional Medal for example, although it is not so extensively awarded. And then there is your military. If I am not mistaken, weren't the medals given to your troops after you invaded Grenada vastly greater than the number of those taking part in the invasion? By the way, now that I think of it, although the Queen is Head of State of Grenada, Britain was not informed of your country's intention to invade it.

I don't know much about that as I wasn't involved. But if it was a pre-emptive strike before Grenada could invade us, then obviously we couldn't tell the Brits or there would have been no surprise. But what I'm really interested in are the honours to entertainment people. Any names I know? Maybe we could do that instead of the Oscars?

Ray Davies was among those who were awarded a CBE.

I know that name. It was on a list of names I was shown last week of Americans who got the Nobel Prize. It's nice that the Brits also recognised him.

The Ray Davis, without the "e", who was co-winner of the Nobel Prize for Physics. is not the same person whose name appears on the British honours list. The CBE went to the Ray Davies who is co-founder of The Kinks.

What the heck is that?

Perhaps that's a question best left unan-swered, or even unasked.

What about the Rolling Stones guy, Mick Jagger, who seems to have been around for a long time? I hear he has suddenly be-come a Sir.

Ah, that was a very special, one might even call it, to use one of your favourite words, a pre-emptive, case. You see, Sir, it was noticed recently that an alarming af-fliction has been spreading among young people in Britain, which the medical pro-fession has named forebear phobia, and which might well spread to other countries if not quickly brought under control.

That sounds just awful. What is it?

It is total aversion to and rejection of their grandfathers. No similar symptoms have been observed when it comes to parents or grandmothers.

How do they become infected?

It wasn't easy but the researchers finally found the root cause but only after the team leader himself became a victim. His granddaughter, instead of greeting him with her usual "Hello, Granddad", suddenly started asking "Do I know you?" when he appeared. His grandson's reaction was even more distressing with "Shove off" replacing his customary warm salutation. He was quite unable to get the young people to explain their behaviour or even to answer when spoken to.

Good grief! Had he done anything to upset them?

Not at all. It was totally beyond explanation. Fortunately he had the good sense to call on his wife for help in finding out what malady their grandchildren were suffering from. At first they were reluctant to talk to her but, after a bit of bribery involving increases in pocket money, they finally confessed to what ailed them. It seems that the youngest people who had been spectators at recent Rolling Stone concerts, or seen them on television, became terrified at the sight of the grandfatherly lead singer, Mick Jagger, gyrating and leaping around the stage like some demented dervish. This gave them terrible nightmares and a subsequent total refusal to have anything to do with the person they identified with what had caused their distress.

What did the researchers have to say about that?

As most of them had last seen the group about 35 years ago, they were a bit sceptical at first, except for the youngest member of the team who had been to a concert in 1980. They had not, therefore, witnessed what one of them later called Mr. Jagger's St. Vitas Prance until they saw a video they had borrowed and were, as the team leader expressed it, left flummoxed by the performance. And that brings me to the honour. It was thought that by giving Mr. Jagger a knighthood he might be persuaded to use his full name and become known as the somewhat more dignified Sir Michael. This should make it harder to continue his on-stage frenzied frolicking and result in more sedate performances in keeping with his senior citizen status.

Then I guess the person finding the cure will also become Sir something, won't he?

Oh, if successful and they are able to stop the scourge from spreading, I should not be surprised if they made him a lord, or even awarded him an Order of Merit which is more prestigious.

I sure hope they find a cure before other countries become infected. Well, I've gotta go now. You know Laura's been after me for ages to help her hang some drapes. So I'll see you again in a couple of days. There are one or two other things I'd like to ask you about.

I too wish the research team success in their efforts. In the meantime all we can do is wait and see and, of course, hope. I look forward to continuing our conversation.

19. A Most Singular Party

Good morning, Mr. President.

Good morning. Today there are a few things I'd like to talk about. First of all, did you see the latest from Al Qaeda? Encouraging, isn't it?

Do you mean their comment that Americans are being chased in the U.S.? I'm afraid I cannot quite see how we can extract anything positive from that remark.

Sure we can. It just shows that even terrorists can be made to appreciate our values. Laura was absolutely thrilled. You know she's very keen on the No Sex Before Marriage movement so she was delighted to learn that even over there they know Americans are learning to be chaste. I sure hope Tony sees it. I really think the Brits should try to take their minds off you know what.

I have to confess, Sir, it never occurred to me to interpret the comments quite in that way. But perhaps it's a sign that progress is being made in at least one direction.

It's a good start. Now I want to ask you about a few things that have been goin' on in England. First of all, I've heard Tony is desperate to get that Mayor guy Livingstone back into the Labour Party. Didn't he throw him out a few years ago? So why would be want him back?

He did indeed get rid of him. Quite brutally. You see, Mr. Livingstone, then a Labour Party member, wanted to stand as the Party's candidate for Mayor of London but Mr. Blair would have none of it. His actual words were that, as Mayor, Mr. Livingstone would be "a disaster for London". So in 2000 he got the Party's National Executive Committee to expel him, for five years as the rules require. As Mr. Livingstone stood as an Independent and won, the Prime Minister is now desperate to get him back to stand as Labour candidate in the next mayoral election.

So how come, if he was a disaster three years ago he is suddenly so great now? And if the rules say he has to be out for five years how can he be brought back so soon?

That's a question many people, including some of Mr. Blair's Cabinet colleagues, are asking. It seems Mr. Blair agrees with

Mr. Bernard Shaw's comment that the golden rule is that there are no golden rules. Some commentators say that adding one more disaster to Mr. Blair's team will not make much difference. It seems the P.M. may have had in mind what one of your predecessors said when explaining American foreign policy that "they may be bastards but they're our bastards" and is applying the same standard to Mr. Livingstone.

So he'll once more be a welcome member of the Labour Party?

I'm not sure it can be said he was ever a member in good standing of the Party. Many believe he cannot be a member of any party since he himself is a party, of one that is.

My guys tell he made a nasty remark about me when he said I made the world a more dangerous place. That just proves what a leftist he is. It's a shame we can't call them Commies any more.

Actually, Sir, that was written by Mr. Clyde Prestowitz, once adviser to President Reagan and now head of the Economic Strategy Institute, the Washington think tank, so it would seem his political leanings are more to the right than to the left. What Mr. Livingstone said was that you are the worst threat to world peace, so it seems on one point at least the right and the left are beginning to converge. But perhaps we should assume that Mr. Livingstone's remark was, as the saying goes, half joking but whole in earnest.

Yeah, it's a gift, isn't it? Bringing people together. But whatever he meant, I'm sure sorry I took him that Touch-It-Up. You don't think he'll use it to change his image when he gets back into the Party?

Oh, I believe Mr. Livingstone's personality would shine through any change of image. As to why Mr. Blair invited him back, rumours have it that he will do anything to take people's minds off Lord Hutton's enquiry report, expected to be published soon.

What's that?

Surely you remember all the fuss about the, excuse my language, sexed-up dossier? And the sad demise of Dr. David Kelly who had warned that the reports of weapons of mass destruction in Iraq were grossly exaggerated, a view now vindicated. The

Hutton enquiry is meant to try to get to the bottom of it.

Sure I remember it. But I heard that when Tony visited the British troops in Iraq he mentioned other weapons we knew nothing about. By the way, I don't think he should have gone there. In my opinion only the Commander-in-Chief should visit the coalition troops and that's me.

Of course you are quite right; it was tactless of him to make that visit. He may think you are not Commander-in-Chief of the British troops. But you see, Sir, Mr. Blair wanted to make his presence felt, again it seems to try to persuade his voters there are things more important than the Hutton report. Besides, as he was on vacation in Egypt he felt that, as it was just around the corner so to speak, he could hop over to Iraq. And he did indeed mention, in his address to the troops, the Weapons of Mass Distraction. Some people suggested he was talking about the weapons used by the coalition but the consensus was that it was a Freudian slip.

Wow! Freud! Isn't he the guy that invented shrinks. There are an awful lot of those in our country I'm sorry to say, mostly in

New York. Maybe some of them could help Tony.

It's a tempting thought, Sir. But I believe psychiatrists can only help those who think they need help and, unhappily, Mr. Blair does not fall into that category.

What I can't understand is why they asked Hutton to make that report. Couldn't they have got someone not so much in the public eye? I remember all that talk years ago about the nude photos. People will only be reminded of them again and it will take their minds off what's in the report. But maybe that was Tony's plan? And then there's that smile.

Good heavens! Nude photographs? That dour Ulsterman? And I am not sure that anyone has ever seen a smile light up the face of the noble lord. Of course, he must have been young once, so who knows? But how on earth has it been kept so quiet?

What Ulsterman?

Lord Hutton.

I really must find time to see that ear man. I thought you said Lauren Hutton.

Tony's conversation with Cherie

I know that expression, Tony, you've been talking to George again. So what is it this time?

He started off by saying he's thinking of establishing a gongs programme. Have you ever heard of such a thing?

No. Maybe he wants to put them in the White House and Camp David to let people like Rumsfeld know when he wants to see them in his office. I think his stay at Buckingham Palace may have gone to his head and now he wants to use a more imperious means of summoning his people. But he can't have called you to tell you just that.

No. He said he's glad neither of us is a grandfather and he hopes they will have found a remedy for the condition before we are.

What condition? Galloping dementia?

Honestly, Cherie, sometimes your remarks are really too much. He also said he's sorry

Mick Jagger has had to be sedated. Did you hear anything about that?

I assumed he always had been, so that is nothing new.

Anyway, George is delighted the latest Al Qaeda video tape shows they have finally seen the light and admitted that the Americans are virtuous.

How is it we didn't hear about that? You're not being passed all the information you should be getting. Didn't Alastair mention it?

You know Alastair Campbell is no longer my director of communications.

But you still keep in close contact with him.

Of course. I call him to congratulate him on anniversaries, birthdays, and so on.

Judging by the number of phone calls he must celebrate all the days of the week. And there must be an awful lot of those multiple birth cases in his family.

Getting back to George. He is very annoyed about my welcoming Livingstone back into the Labour Party.

That's a nice way of expressing your begging him to come back to the fold to stand as candidate for the post you thought he'd be a calamity in the last time.

I'd hardly say that. I just think it would be uncharitable not to extend a hand to him when he obviously wants to rejoin his old friends.

If he wants to be with his old friends, why does he want to come back to the Party? Well, let's hope he wins. If he doesn't it really will be a calamity. But is that all George had to say about him?

He said he was glad Ken was turning towards the right. News to me I must say but it would be nice if we could at least nudge him a little bit towards a more measured stance.

That would be an advance. Then, instead of being known as the leader of the loony left he could be called the skipper of the screwball centre.

Another thing. Have you ever heard mention of anyone known as Holy Ernest?

No. Is he some religious leader in the news? A Billy Graham man, perhaps? Maybe he's one of George's fundamentalists or evangelists or whatever they're called. Didn't he ever mention him during your prayer sessions? I'm sure there's no Ernest among the Anglican hierarchy, at least I've never heard of one.

Despite what the papers say, we never had any....oh, never mind. What about the Catholics. You must know all about them.

I don't know them all but the name Ernest definitely rings a bell. Wasn't there a Bishop Ernest something or other in the news a few years ago? Now I remember, it was Bishop Ernest Kombo, from the Congo if my memory serves me. He was one of those who, at a meeting with the Pope, said they thought nuns should be appointed to the College of Cardinals so that they could have a say in choosing His Holiness's successor.

That must have gone down well with Pope John Paul.

He made no comment at the meeting, but I was told by a contact in the Curia, an Irish Jesuit, that when it was over he expressed himself very forcefully in language that was far from pontifical. Luckily it was in Latin with such a strong Polish accent that hardly anyone present could make

out what he was on about. But is that all
he had to say?

*No, indeed. He mentioned the Hutton en-
quiry and said he really didn't understand
what it was about but he was glad he was
mistaken about the nude photos.*

Oh good lord! Or not, as the case may be.
Surely not Hutton, the prim and proper Law
Lord. I can't believe it.

*Amazing, isn't it? Who would have
thought? I hope to heaven nothing about
that gets out. Imagine the publicity. We
could never live it down.*

You know, Tony. It might not be so bad if
word did get out. Just think. Although you
fully expect to be totally exonerated from
any blame, if the report does not treat you
as gently as you hope, it might not be a
bad idea to have something like that up
your sleeve to let fall at the right moment.

*Honestly, Cherie, you can't be serious. I
don't think for a moment there's anything
in it. The austere, upright, uncompromis-
ing Lord Hutton. Of all people! No, I simply
can't credit it. It's just too preposterous.
Besides, whatever it was, George said he
was mistaken.*

Well, he would, wouldn't he? He probably realized he had let slip something he shouldn't have. Don't forget what they say about still waters running deep.

And it is into those deep waters that you would like me to plunge, head first I suppose. No, I think we should just ignore it and hope nothing will leak.

That nothing will leak from that sieve known as the White House is really too much to hope for. It is obviously built of the same porous material as the royal palaces.

20. Everything You've Always Wanted To Know

Good morning, Mr. President.

Well, hi. You've been away a long time. Visiting back home, I guess.

Yes, Sir. I feel I have to make an extended visit from time to time. There's nothing like being on the spot to get up to date with what's going on.

A pity you missed my State of the Union address.

I assure you Sir, I made a point of watching it on TV.

They showed the whole thing on British television?

Yes, indeed. Now that the United Kingdom is an honorary U.S. state, British television gives extensive coverage to all your pronouncements. You now appear much more often than Mr. Blair, especially on the BBC. Unfortunately, I was called away for a short while so I missed what you had to say about your earlier promise to send a man to Mars and your comments on the Middle East road map.

I didn't mention either of those items. I concentrated on things that really matter so I talked about the use of steroids in sport and the sanctity of marriage.

Yes, of course. As head of state you must pay attention to the vital interests of the nation. When people start using steroids heaven only knows what appalling, even terrorist, acts might follow. Did you consult Mr. Schwarzenegger about the use of steroids?

Heck, no. Now that he's Governor I thought it might be tactless.

What is important is that you made your views known. I was surprised to hear you think the Constitution should be amended to preclude any possibility of marriage between couples of the same sex.

Why did that surprise you?

Because amendments to the Constitution sometimes lead to confusion when people interpret them in different ways.

How could it lead to confusion? It's God's law that marriage has to be between a man and a woman and no-one should be allowed to transgress that law.

I have to confess that it never occurred to me that being a marriage broker is among the Almighty's many responsibilities, but I do think misunderstandings might arise. If the Constitution is to declare the sanctity of marriage, will divorce be outlawed, or will it still be permitted so long as those who divorce are branded as sinners? And what will happen to adulterers? I do not think a scarlet letter would go down too well nowadays. Then too, might not such an amendment give offence to the Republican gays, of whom there suddenly seem to be a great many more than anyone ever suspected?

Now you mustn't get me wrong. As I keep saying, I have nothing against gays — I even have some working on my re-election campaign — and it's not my business what people do when they're alone in their own homes. But gay marriage is out.

Will that not upset Mrs. Bush?

Why should it? I hope you're not implying she's that way inclined.

Oh, certainly not, Sir! What I mean is, as you told me that Mrs. Bush is a strong supporter of the No Sex Before Marriage, or maybe it is No Sex Without Marriage Movement, will she not be upset that you think it is all right for gays to have sex without being married while everyone else is being admonished not to have sex unless they get married?

Gee, I never thought about that. Why didn't Dick mention it

Mr. Cheney, Sir? I had no idea he is an expert on the subject although I am aware of his very close family connections to people of that persuasion. Perhaps that will make it hard for him to go along with your suggested amendment?

I don't know about that but, because of his contacts, he's the guy who's supposed to let me know what's going on in that direction. I can't understand why an amendment to the Constitution should cause any confusion. So what the heck is all the fuss about?

I was thinking there might be a similar problem to that caused by how some people interpret the second amendment about the right to bear arms.

I've never understood all that to-do. It's clear as daylight.

As I understand it, the problem is that a lot of people do not believe, or claim they do not believe, that the right to bear arms refers to a people's collective militia and not to people as individuals.

That's one of the dumbest things I've ever heard. That right sure as heck does not apply to the militia or to any of the other people whose job it is to defend us. Can you imagine what a militia or an army would look like with bare arms? Mighty silly. I say everyone except the militia should have a right to bare arms. And I have no problem with bare legs either, though I must say I never approved of those hot pants that were popular years ago. I think they went too far.

Mr. President, you have certainly made me see the second amendment in a new light. As to the hot pants, I always thought the complaint about them was that they didn't go far enough.

Anyway, I'm getting sick and tired of all the talk about sex, especially the gays who are causing us so much trouble. By the way, I can't imagine why they call themselves gay; some I've come across are anything but. I never knew what the heterosexuals were until someone told me they are normal people like you and me so I don't see why they can't just say so. What I don't get are the bisexuals. How the heck can anyone be two sexes at the same time?

Bisexual does not mean people who have two sexes at the same time. They would be ambisexuals and are quite different and also much rarer than bisexuals. In fact normal people, just like you and me, who are not ambisexual can be, and sometimes are, bisexual. But perhaps these are technicalities we should not pursue.

And I used to think sex was so simple. Just to be on the safe side, and so that people don't get the wrong idea, I never go to a barbershop unless it has a unisex sign in the window.

Indeed, Mr. President, one cannot be too careful.

You seem to know a lot about it, so tell me if there are any other new sexes I may not have heard of.

I can claim no expertise but I confess I do read newspapers and magazines, a practice I know you disapprove of. If I may, I would like to suggest you try it occasionally. As to your question, in addition to homosexual, bisexual and heterosexual, terms I have seen mentioned are pansexual, polysexual, transsexual, perisexual and omnisexual some of which, as far as I can determine, are simply different ways of describing the same thing.

It used to be so simple when there were only two sexes. I'm not sure about the newspapers. I'd have to ask my three car guys what they think.

As you say, it is a shame that the good old days when men were men and women were women are no longer with us. But who are your car guys, Mr. President? Surely you do not ride in a car pool?

A president couldn't do that. They're not car, c-a-r guys. They're C period A period R period guys. Cheney, Ashcroft, Rumsfeld. I call them that because if I mention one the other two get real sore, and I'm sick and tired of always having to say the three names. Anyway now that people have so many multiple choices about sex it must make it very hard for them to make up their minds.

Yes, indeed, Sir. If your triumvirate does agree that you may read a magazine or two, be prepared to see mention of the metrosexuals that are suddenly appearing among us.

Retrosexuals. That sounds real depraved.

Oh, dear, I really must be careful of my enunciation. The word I said was metrosexuals, with an "m".

I might have known it. The French again. But heck, you shouldn't worry about renunciation so long as you don't cross state lines, if you get my meaning.

Oh, I do Sir, and I thank you for your advice. You may rest assured I have always taken great pains to keep on the right side of the railway, I mean railroad, track. But the name has nothing to do with the Paris subway system. It describes a trend that first saw the light of day in London.

The Brits. What can you expect? They can't take their minds off it, can they? No wonder the Puritans had to leave the place. I guess they couldn't stand it any more. But what do these metrosexuals do? I bet they get up to some pretty weird shenanigans. Or perhaps I shouldn't ask.

As I understand it, they are not known for actually doing anything in particular, they just are. As to their behaviour, I have not heard that they engage in any practices peculiar to themselves. In fact, in spite of the name, there is no reason why a metro-sexual could not also be asexual.

As what?

As what what, Sir?

You just said they could be as sexual but you didn't say as what?

What I meant was they might be sexless.

No sex? Then maybe I should put them in touch with Laura. The more people join the Movement the better. What do you think?

I am not sure if that is such a good idea. While some of them might have no sex, others can be hypersexual. Indeed, that is a claim made about their most popular role model.

195

What are women metrosexuals called?

There are no women metrosexuals.   Or rather, women are said to be natural, genetically programmed, metrosexuals.

Just what you'd expect.   That's why I don't want any of our guys foolin' around with genes. I only hope weirdoes like that don't start trying to get onto our D.C. metro trains.

I do not think you need worry about that. I have the feeling that while New York might be a target, the inhabitants of Washington, D.C. will never have to suffer an attack of the metrosexuals.

I don't think New York could take another hit so I better rush off and alert our Homeland Security people. I hope to see you when I get back from my upcoming trip overseas. I'm sure looking forward to visiting that castle in Ireland. I'm told the Irish always give their visitors a hundred thousand welcomes. Is that true?

I too look forward to our next meeting. As to the Irish, they are indeed known for warmly receiving guests, especially American presidents.   When President Clinton went there the axiom about the 100,000 welcomes was proven to be true when that many people poured onto the Dublin streets to cheer and shout his name. I think it is safe to assume they will greet you as no other U.S. president has ever been greeted in their country.

21. The Law's DeLay

Good morning, Mr. President.

Good morning, nice to see you.

I hope you have recovered from your trip to Ireland and Turkey.

Yes, thanks, I really enjoyed it. Especially surprising everyone when we handed over Iraq to the Iraqis before we said we would. Although when I told Tony, before anyone else of course, his mind seemed to be elsewhere. And it's not the first time that's happened.

What makes you think Mr. Blair was not paying attention?

He suddenly said he loves ducks. It was probably to show me he's gotten over his hatred of birds.

That may well be but I suspect there is another explanation. His mind might have been on the Butler report due in a couple of days or he might have been thinking about his next meal. Still, I believe what he said was "Love a duck!" an English expression used when someone is taken aback at unexpected news.

What's the butler report? Something dreamed up by one of those Palace guys who now write their memoirs?

No, Sir, it is a report by Lord Butler on the Iraq affair, including Mr. Blair's dodgy dossier.

Didn't they just have a report on that by another lord?

Yes, they did, Sir, by Lord Hutton. But the public was so sceptical about the first lord's report on his enquiry that they decided to get a second lord's opinion. There were also two other enquiries, so this is the fourth.

They seem to have an awful lot of enquiries over there.

They do indeed. Some members of Parliament want an enquiry into why there are so many enquiries but, so far, no lord has been named to head it. But getting back to Mr. Blair's surprise, I am sure he was not the only person caught off guard, especially by Mr. Paul Bremer's hasty withdrawal.

He's a modest guy. He didn't want the Iraqis to make a fuss and give him a great send-off with big bands and all.

In some quarters it is being said that, expecting he might be sent off with big bangs, he did what the British call a moonlit flit.

They got that wrong. He left in broad daylight.

Of course he did. A sort of high noon getaway.

Well, now they've got their own government. Isn't that what they wanted?

Just the government they wanted. But Sir, if I may, I'd like to forget about Iraq for a moment. So many other things have been happening. For example, the long delayed arrest of the Enron CEO Mr. Kenneth Lay. Do you think he will be found guilty of any infraction?

I can't comment on that. I was never able to get the hang of any kind of fractions.

Then maybe they will find him guilty of wrongdoing?

No way. Didn't you see him on Larry King when he explained he knew nothing about what was going on?

I remember the days when people at the top were supposed to know what was going on and took responsibility when things went wrong. President Truman, for example, with his the buck stops here.

Don't forget, he was a Democrat.

Yes, of course. And then you have to face the DeLay problem.

I've told you before, when all the problems started I broke off contact with Lay, at least in public, so I don't care how long they delay.

No, Sir, I do not mean the Lay delay. I mean the problem of DeLay.

Do you feel O.K.?

Yes Sir, thank you. I am referring to Mr. Tom DeLay, the House Majority Leader, who is also mentioned in connection with Enron when he solicited funds from them for what he called the Party's redistricting effort in Texas. Gerrymandering.

Never heard of him. The only Jerry I know is Falwell whose Moral Majority does a great fund raising job for us.

The term comes from a former governor of Massachusetts whose name was Gerry.

Massachusetts. Then you mean Kerry. I might have known.

No, Sir, I am talking about Gerry with a G and he was long before Mr. Kerry's time, about 200 years. He devised a scheme to manipulate and redraw election districts so that his party would have an unfair advantage. The name is derived from the appearance of the first district so manipulated which had the shape of a salamander.

That guy must have been a Republican. By the way, what's a salamander?

Yes, Sir, as far as I know he was. As to salamander, just think newt.

I haven't heard much about him lately. I wonder what he's doing?

Mr. Newt Gingrich, Sir? I really cannot say. But to get back to the gerrymandering skills of Mr. DeLay, he used and still uses them to ensure that practically all the votes in Texas go to the Republican Party.

So what's to complain about?

Nothing at all, except that the practice is illegal and Mr. DeLay and his colleagues are facing lawsuits and an investigation by a criminal prosecutor.

Maybe Ken Lay can arrange for him to go on the Larry King show to explain every-thing.

Good thinking, Sir. That should clear away any doubts anyone might still have about his guilt. There is something else I would like to bring up.

Just go ahead. You know you can ask me anything you like.

It is concerning the AIDS conference in Bangkok. Has there been any change in the U.S. position that the best way to deal with the disease is the Say No to Sex ap-proach?

There sure as heck hasn't been any change. I don't know why people get so hot and bothered about it.

They probably know that statistics show drug use went up after Mrs. Reagan's Say No to Drugs campaign was launched.

I can tell you it's not easy to say no to drugs.

Well you should know, Sir. But of course you now find it is easier to abstain than most people who are not fortunate enough to have been born again. And then when it comes to saying no to sex few people have your great inspiration.

What do you mean? What inspiration is that?

Mrs. Bush, Sir. Her Movement that is. It must provide you with great motivation.

Well, gee, thanks. I guess.

We must not forget there are great dangers inherent in any Say No effort. An example is a recent attempt in Britain to launch just such a campaign with results that can only be described as calamitous. The news was given to me in the strictest confidence but I am mentioning it because I believe you have a right to be kept in the picture.

That it failed is no surprise. From what I know of the Brits you'll never get them to say no to sex.

It was not sex, Sir. The fact is, they have developed a very serious weight problem. The increase in obesity has been such that they are in danger of beating your own country when it comes to competing in the avoirdupois stakes.

What can they expect if they keep on stuffin' themselves with those exploding sausages? But they'll never beat us in the stakes you mentioned 'cos you can bet your bottom dollar we'll never enter any of those French horse races. By the way, that reminds me of when I was at the tavern with Tony and Cherie. I though the French were the only ones who ate frogs so I was shocked to see that the daily special was toad-in-the-hole. I could hardly believe my eyes.

I can assure you, Sir, the British dish is a native one made with the same ingredients as their much loved sausages, with the explosive element removed of course. It has a totally different taste and texture from the French grenouilles. As to the weight problem, the National Health Service is now spending so much on obesity-related diseases that they set out to try to find a remedy.

What did they do?

The Ministry of Health conducted a trial, some say at the instigation of the Minister himself while others claim it was the idea of a senior civil servant. They asked for volunteers, men and women, to join in their Just Say No test. Mind you, it was not easy to persuade people to take part but, as you know, as there are always those willing to try anything they finally got together a group of twelve.

What did they have to say no to? I suppose bread and potatoes for a start?

The Ministry decided drastic, or what in Texas you would call cold turkey, measures were needed so the members of the trial group were told to Say No to Food. They could drink as much water as they liked.

Wow! And did it work?

Absolutely! The results were quite dramatic. In no time at all the corpulent figures of those in the group became quite svelte, not to say skeletal. The success of the experiment could not be doubted.

It's strange we haven't heard about it in the U.S. And Tony never mentioned it. We could sure use some remedy like that here. I can hardly sit anywhere any more without some tub of lard dropping down beside me.

I sympathize. And we should not forget how often excessively stout figures indicate a health risk and a diminished ability to perform their tasks.

You mean a fatso might not be able to do his job properly?

That is certainly one way of putting it.

Now let me get this straight. Are you saying a guy who's overweight, someone in a position where decisions have to be made, could be dumped, I mean fired?

I am not sure whether the labour law would allow that. But there would be no obligation to renew such a person's contract.

For example, someone like, for instance....?

An example might be a senior person like a manager or even a vice-president.

You don't say! Even a vice-president? It's a pity U.S. vice-presidents don't have contracts. About the trial. What was the final result?

Unfortunately, Sir, the trial had to be abandoned because of a very grave, and totally unforeseen, side effect.

What was that?

I am afraid it was the group's demise.

Well, that's not too serious. We had the same problem with some of our people, including Cheney and Rumsfeld.

Good heavens! I had no idea. When? As to not being serious, I am sure you are the best judge.

I don't know when it started. Years ago, I guess. They corrected it by getting great eyeglasses so it's no longer a problem.

Oh, now I understand why what they kept seeing in Iraq were the WDMs instead of WMDs. It was due to their dim eyes.

I never knew they saw WDMs. Why wasn't I told? And are they more lethal than the WMDs?

The WDMs are the Widely Dispersed Mirages and they turned out to be very lethal indeed. But I am talking about another type of demise. The type where those affected kick the bucket.

If some darn fool hadn't put the bucket there in the first place, they couldn't have kicked it, could they?

You are quite right, Sir. What I meant was that they shuffled off this mortal coil; in other words, they died or, as you would put it, they passed.

That sure as heck is one condition nothing can be done to change.

Unfortunately not. Mind you, attempts were made. Experts were called in from Haiti, the only country where they have had some degree of success in reversing the condition. But to no avail. It seems the remedy is only effective when applied in Haiti and to natives of the country.

*I always thought they were pretty back-
ward in Haiti and now you tell me they've
made great advances in medicine.*

Yes, but only in that particular area in
which they are specialists.

*What did the people think? Weren't they
alarmed when they were told the whole
group had passed on?*

The truth could not be told so the Ministry said a group of people had been infected by a hitherto unknown virus that
caused an irreversible wasting disease. To
calm fears, they also said they are coming close to developing a vaccine. But,
Sir, I must beg you to keep this entirely to
yourself. I could get into very hot water if it
ever came out that I had divulged it, even
to you.

*I won't tell a soul. You've got such great
information sources it's a pity you're not a
U.S. citizen so that you could join our intelligence service. They sure could do with
your input.*

Thank you, Mr. President, for those kind
words. I only hope the little information I

can pass on to you is of some assistance, even if it must be kept strictly confidential.

It sure is. Next time I'd like to ask you about the new report. You know we had our own report, don't you?

Yes, I do know, Sir, and I look forward to learning what conclusions were reached.

Tony's conversation with Cherie

Well, Tony, recovered from your trip to Turkey? Your pal's handing over Iraq to the Iraqis so early caught everyone off guard.

Yes, it did, didn't it? I was quite surprised myself when I heard it was to happen like that. But I thought it odd that Paul Bremer fled the scene without even waiting for Negroponte to arrive.

Well, wouldn't anyone? Apart from Iraq, has George had anything interesting to tell you since he got back to Washington? It's been ages since you've passed on his words of wisdom.

Not really. He harped back to his State of the Union message and rambled on about keeping people from using steroids in sports. Oh, and maintaining the sanctity of marriage. Then, apropos of absolutely nothing, he told me he has no intention of sending U.S. forces off to battle improperly dressed — something about making sure they are well covered up.

Maybe the troops have been complaining about the heat in Iraq and the heavy gear they have to carry.

I have no idea. But getting back to the marriage business, he claims that, although some of his best friends are gays and he doesn't care what they do, he wants to make sure the Constitution prohibits them from marrying one another.

I thought a lot of them had already done that, so isn't it a bit late?

Yes they have, in some states. But if marriage between persons of the same sex is forbidden by the U.S Constitution it will apply all over the country and the states won't have any say in the matter. In any case, although he claims to be fed up with all the talk about sex he made a comment that really blew my mind. I can tell you it was the last thing I'd expect to hear from him, or anyone else for that matter.

Well, don't leave me all agog. What was it?

From what I could make out, he's very concerned about his lay problems.

Tony, he never said anything of the kind! You obviously misheard. He said gay problems, which is what he'd been talking about.

I thought so too, but he not only repeated it, he went on to say something that left me speechless.

Again? If it so impressed you it must have been something mind blowing. So, what was it?

You hit the nail on the head. It really did blow my mind. He complained that the delay problem is what is causing him sleepless nights. I can't imagine why he mentioned it to me. Shouldn't he be consulting Bob Dole about that?

Well yes, as he's the one who plugs Viagra on the tele he would seem to be the logical choice. But I expect George feels that, ever since he anointed, I mean appointed, you First Chum there's nothing sacred and he can confide his most intimate secrets to you.

I tell you I felt quite uncomfortable, especially as he went on to ask me what I knew about the new sexes they've invented. He

seemed to hint we are the ones responsi-
ble because he said he hopes we can do
something to keep the subway sex guys
away from New York.

I suppose by subway he means the underground. It's true one occasionally sees
what might be described as unaccept-
able behaviour on the tube, especially on
the Piccadilly Line, but I suspect no more
so than in New York.

No, it can't be that. I did ask him if he was
talking about the tube but he couldn't
have been paying attention because he
said not much could be done about tel-
evision. He mentioned the AIDS Confer-
ence in Bangkok and still insists that the
best way to prevent AIDS is to stop people
from having sex.

That should please Laura. Maybe the No
Sex Without Marriage Movement she supports is influencing the U.S. position. Or is it
the No Marriage Without Sex Movement?

Honestly Cherie, I don't think the Move-
ment is anything like you make it out to
be. Anyway, George expressed great re-
gret that our Just Say No campaign had
failed. I must confess I never knew we had
one.

Neither did I. But he must have said more than that.

No, when I asked him what he meant all he said was I could rely on him to keep the secret. He then totally changed the subject, suggesting we keep away from French race tracks and stop toadying up to them. Have we been, toadying up to the French I mean?

Not that I know of. The only thing I can think of is that he probably wants to stop you getting too close to Kerry, his Democratic opponent, with his French connections. What else could it be?

Oh, and he seemed to be quite chuffed to find out that a heterosexual is a normal person just like him.

An oxymoron if ever I heard one. But anything else on what seems to have become his favourite subject?

He reeled off a whole list of the new sexes he says have been discovered, and of which I've never heard. He seems to think we invented them. He doesn't read, so I can't imagine where he gets his information. One thing he said about our non-existent Just Say No campaign is that we shouldn't give up on Haiti. He plans to visit that country the next time he has time off. He says he wants to see what progress they've made in their medical specialty. What could he possibly mean?

I haven't a clue but there's one thing you can be absolutely sure of.

May I ask what that is?

In the land of the zombies, he won't feel at all out of place.

22. What's in a Name?

Good morning Mr. President. Please accept my congratulations on your election.

Oh, hi. Good to see you again. It's been a long time. Thanks, but I think you mean my re-election.

Yes, quite. It has indeed been a long time, Sir. But in the last months you have had little time to talk, what with campaign and all. And, of course, a lot has happened in the meantime.

Yeah, I'm sure glad that's over although it was well worth it. And now that I've got Condi over at State I think we'll be able to fix whatever is still wrong with the world.

I have no doubt the world will be relieved to hear that. There is one thing about Dr. Rice's remarks that has left many people puzzled.

What could that be? I thought she made everything perfectly clear.

It was her comment that some countries, including North Korea and Iran, are outposts of tyranny. It seems to clash with your classification of them as an axis of evil

I can't see what the problem is.

Some people cannot understand how they can be at the centre as an axis and at the same time be on the fringe as outposts. Maybe you could explain in your next press conference?

I'd rather let Condi do that. You know she does have a way with words, and she sure has a lot of them. Now, what was it we were we talking about when we last met?

I believe you asked about the two reports by Lord Hutton and Lord Butler on Mr. Blair's dodgy dossier. How long ago it all seems!

It sure does. But what did the reports finally say?

Lord Hutton found, as I think I may have mentioned before, that many mistakes were made but no-one made them, the same words that Mr. Alastair Campbell, the Prime Minister's spokesman, had used. Lord Butler, on the other hand, discovered that many people were to blame but no-one was culpable.

And they say Tony came out clean as a whistle.

Yes indeed he did, Sir. But Mr. Blair's ability to dodge the bullet has led to confusion in certain quarters. One of England's most popular young actors was furious when he found out, on being offered the part of the Artful Dodger, that it was the secondary character based on Dickens' novel instead of, as the name would suggest, the lead role in a play about the Prime Minister.

There's no doubt Tony's had his share of problems. All that business when the Home Secretary resigned. Poor Dave. I guess the Brits wouldn't put up with a Cabinet Minister having an illicit affair.

A British Cabinet Minister having an illicit affair is hardly unknown and would not cause a ripple among the public. Mr. Blunkett felt he had to go because, first of all, he let his lover, Mrs. Kimberly Quinn, use a fast track to get a nanny into the country. And then there was the matter of the misuse of public transport funds.

Gee, I sure sympathize about the nanny. I've had that problem twice. With Bernard Kerik, who could not take the Homeland Security job, and then with Linda Chavez who had to turn down Labour, because they both had employed illegal immigrants as nannies.

Mrs. Quinn's nanny was in the country quite legally. It was just that Mr. Blunkett rushed her application through.

And that's a crime? It sure was a mistake to misuse public transport funds. How much are we talking about? In dollars, please, pounds always confuse me.

Let me see. I do not know exactly, but I believe it was in region of 350.

And to think of all the fuss everyone made about the little Halliburton slip up when they charged for food they never delivered and overcharged for gasoline. I don't think that even came to 200 million dollars but maybe they're right to make an uproar about 350 million.

Oh no, Sir. I did not make myself clear. The sum was 350 dollars, not 350 million dollars. It was the cost of a couple of train tickets from London to Doncaster that

Mr. Blunkett let Mrs. Quinn use, although they were meant for use by a spouse.

I get it. As Mrs. Quinn is not a spouse she shouldn't have used them.

Actually she is a spouse, but someone else's. Her use of the tickets caused considerable surprise, not to say bewilderment, in Britain and utter amazement in Europe.

Why was that?

The British could not think of any reason why anyone who was not a native of the town would want to go to Doncaster, except of course to see the famous St. Leger horse race and it was confirmed that the trips were not taken at that time. On the continent they were flabbergasted that giving anyone a ticket to travel by rail in Britain could possibly be considered a favour. The consensus there was that giving her the tickets was a sure sign Mr. Blunkett wanted to end the affair.

How did news of the nanny and the tickets get out?

Mrs. Quinn, who as a magazine publisher has many contacts among journalists, wrote a kiss-and-tell story in a daily news-paper.

That seems kinda mean to me.

Indeed, if a man had been guilty of such dastardly behaviour he would have been branded a cad and the papers would be flooded with letters to the editor calling for him to be horsewhipped.

I guess they couldn't do that to a woman.

No, Sir, the main problem was what to call her. Cadette, spelt c-a-d-e-t-t-e, was suggested but the Girl Guides, the name Girl Scouts are called over there, protested because, though spelt differently, it could easily be confused with their leaders or cadets. Then caddee, spelt c-a-d-d-e-e, was put forward, but then the members of the British Golf Caddies Association were up in arms about that for the same reason. I made my own suggestion to a couple of editors that a female cad should be called a fad, but I am afraid they were not at all receptive of the idea. So, as no-one could decide what she should be called, she simply got away with it and all the condemnation was directed at the unfortunate Home Secretary.

Why didn't they have an enquiry, as they always do?

Oh, there was one, Mr. President, an in-depth enquiry by Sir Alan Blunt which, by all accounts, took him at least half an hour.

Only a sir. Didn't they have any lord to spare?

As the Prime Minister was not involved I believe it was thought a lord would be overdoing it. And Sir Alan found there was nothing to enquire about.

Who would've thought a proper English gal could behave like that?

She's not English, Sir. Mrs. Quinn is American, from California.

Oh, well, California, that says it all! But say, I hear you're leaving soon. Is that so?

Yes, Sir, I'm afraid it is. The powers that be have given me another assignment. They want me to look at how things are going in other parts of the world like Iraq, Afghanistan, Iran and such places. But I'll be back in Washington one of these days and, if you will permit me, I would be glad to give you a first-hand report.

Gee, thanks. I'd appreciate that. I've enjoyed our little chats and now I know an awful lot more about the Brits and their funny way of talking. By the way, I've never told anyone else what we discuss and my people are always astonished at how well I understand Tony. Maybe you will be in Iraq when we have our victory parade and you can join in.

Yes, I may well be assigned to Iraq to cover the winning side's victory parade. Sir, I cannot say goodbye without expressing my thanks for the privilege, as a foreigner, of being allowed to get a glimpse of an American president's thought process. All I can say is it has been an experience that at times has left me utterly discombobulated.

I don't know how you always manage to find just the right word.

Epilogue

Oh hi, they told me you were back again.

Good morning, Mr. President.

It's sure good to see you. Not many people stop over nowadays. Even Bob Woodward, who I could never get rid of, hasn't been seen lately. I wonder what he's up to.

Preparing his new book or pontificating on a lecture tour I expect. Sir, I am sorry to say I'm only in Washington on a very brief visit. My paper is sending me to South America to report on the sudden climate change. I just stopped by to pay my respects.

Gee, thanks. But don't believe all that talk about global warming. It's a plot to try to make us give up our SUVs. So they might be sending you off on a wild goose chase.

What my bosses have in mind is the change in the political climate rather than the temperature. But perhaps we can talk a little about what has been happening here.

A lot of water has flowed over the bridge since we last met. Big changes, but not only here, over there too I'm told. Berlusconi gone, just like Aznar. They tell me the guy who beat José is a shoemaker. I wonder how he got into politics?

It's true Mr. Zapatero's name means shoemaker, but that was never his profession. As to changes, I have heard a lot of your people have gone over the bridge with the water, including your spokesman or press secretary and the CIA director. And then there are the changes that were not of your making.

Such as?

Mr. David Abramoff, for example.

Who`s he?

Until recently the most powerful and high profile Republican lobbyist in Washington known, I have been told, as the King of K Street.

Never heard of him. But what happened to him?

I believe he is waiting to serve his time in prison after being found guilty of fraud.

Even the laudatory letters written by hundreds of members of his family and friends saying he is a really nice religious guy who never takes his hat off and hates Communism did not save him.

I guess every barrel has one rotten apple.

I understand some other apples in the Republican barrel have been found to be seriously damaged, for example Mr. Randy Duke Cunningham now in prison for fraud and tax evasion. Then there are the questions hanging over the heads of Mr. Tom DeLay, Mr. Karl Rove, and others.

I'm sure they have a perfectly good explanation for everything they're supposed to have done.

I am sure they do. I understand the recently fired CIA director Mr. Porter Goss, and his assistant Mr. Kyle Foggo, are also under scrutiny, as are the odd hookergate goings on at the Watergate Hotel. I think it strange that Mr. Woodward has kept mum about that subject since he always had, and still has, so much to say about Watergate. I'm also told a lot of people were expecting you to replace Mr. Snow.

Now why the heck would I do that when I've just appointed him?

I mean Mr. John Snow your Treasury Secretary, not Mr. Tony Snow your new spokesman. By the way, I am told that appointment caused some surprise.

Why should people be surprised?

Maybe they wonder why you would choose someone who called you an embarrassment and impotent.

He must have meant Bob Dole who, as you know, is the Viagra guy. What's so great about Tony Snow is that he knows how to talk and they say that can be an asset in a mouthpiece. Oh shucks, I mustn't forget I'm supposed to call him a spokesperson or press secretary. But maybe having two Snows might confuse some people. I'll have to think about it.

Yes, having two many snows around when things are beginning to melt could be quite dangerous. But getting back to Mr. Abramoff, others close to him are being tarred with the same brush.

Who might they be?

The person most mentioned is his tailor. Rumour has it that the President of the International Tailors' Guild is accusing him of committing the most heinous sartorial offences. And then you had to deal with Vice-President Cheney's mishap when he shot his friend instead of a quail.

A lot of fuss was made about that. It was a mistake anyone could make.

Hunting accidents do happen. What puzzled people I think is that Mr. Cheney did not notice the quail was orange and was on the ground instead of in flight and, of course, was considerably larger than quails usually are. But, of course, it was a Texan quail.

Poor Dick, he was really hurt about it.

Though not, I imagine, as much as his friend. Even worse is Mr. Kenneth Lay's recent demise which was unfortunate, though some have called it fortuitous.

I don't know about that but it sure was a great bit of luck.

Well, Sir, I cannot quite see where the good luck comes in.

Sure you can. If he had lived until they sentenced him he would have had to pay back all the money they say he stole from Enron. Now his family can keep it. But tell me about Tony. I hear he's also made some changes. As he's no longer on the phone every five minutes like he used to be I'm not in the picture. And the Conservatives have a new leader.

Yes, Mr. David Cameron now heads the Conservative Party and Mr. Blair has indeed made some cabinet changes. The most unexpected was to remove Mr. Jack Straw, the Foreign Secretary, and make him Leader of the House of Commons. While some people think it was sensible, it caused great surprise to many.

I may have had something to do with that. I told our Ambassador over there I would not tolerate any foreign minister who said I was nuts, and he passed it on to Tony.

I believe his use of the word nuts referred to any plan to invade Iran. But it is a shame he went after he and Dr. Rice became so close. Visits to one another's home towns and of course he did sleep in her bed on that plane.

Good grief! I know British ministers like to engage in what you would call hanky-panky but I won't have them doing it with my people. I can hardly believe it. Condi! She's the last person I'd ever expect to carry on like that. It only goes to show.

Sir, let me assure you Dr. Rice was not in her bed at the time. She slept on the floor, which many thought extraordinarily self-sacrificing.

She must have seen the Da Vinci Code movie.

It had not come out yet but she may have read the book. She did admit the Americans had made an awful lot of mistakes in Iraq, many thought at Mr. Straw's instigation.

Well, he had no darn business instigating her. But what about that Prescott guy, his Vice President. Tony didn't get rid of him did he?

No, Sir, Mr. Blair kept Mr. Prescott as his Deputy although he relieved him of all his responsibilities while letting him keep his salary, official residences and cars.

Could he do that, even though he was having an affair with someone in his office? Didn't people complain?

The affair in itself did not bother many people. What bothered them is that he turned his office into a love nest. Still, it probably explained why he needed two Jaguar cars, one for official trips and the other for, well, other activities. However, a lot of people were glad they at last found out what he was doing. Before all this came out few people had any idea about what a Deputy Prime Minister did.

I guess all this means poor Tony is having the same problems with the Poles' opinion. I always thought they were our friends and now they seem to have turned against us. I can't understand why so many people pay so much attention to them.

Well, Mr. President, the polls only reflect how people's views have changed so they are very important to any politician, especially when elections are on the horizon. People do take a lot of notice of them.

Don't they have enough problems of their own without butting into ours. A pity they got rid of that Lech Walesa guy. He was my dad's great friend you know. I'm sure he'd have put a stop to all this nonsense.

I'm afraid I don't quite....... oh yes I see. I believe you are right, Sir, he probably would. But they do always express what people are thinking and they will go on doing so. I am afraid there is little that can be done to stop them. I expect your thoughts are now turning to the next Presidential election in 2008?

Yeah, once we get over the mid-term elections this year I've got to give some thought to 2008, especially about who should be the Republication nominee.

You are not thinking of running again, Mr. President?

You should know I can't do that. A president can only be elected twice.

That is something to which I have been giving some thought. While you were elected in 2004, if I am not mistaken in 2000 you were appointed by the Supreme Court so, technically, since the Court stopped the re-count you have only been elected once and not re-elected. So why should you not run again in 2008 for your second election?

You're real smart. I don't know what the guys in the Party would think of it.

Oh, I am sure they would be glad to see how a sitting president can run.

If I do decide to have another go, could I persuade you to head up my re-election committee?

Thank you for the suggestion, Sir, it would be a real honour. But I am afraid that would not be possible. I have commitments for the next couple of years. Besides, your people might resent a foreigner being part of such a delicate enterprise.

I guess you're right. I better call John Roberts at the Supreme Court to start the ball rolling. He owes me. There's just one thing bothering me. It's Jeb. He's sure gonna be disappointed.

But, Sir, I thought your brother was not interested in carrying on the dynasty.

Didn't you hear him say he was not ruling in or out running for president? Who knows what he's got up his sleeve.

In any case, I firmly believe you must put family feelings aside and, as a predecessor of yours said, think what you can do for your country. What better service could you render than to continue for another four years? Perhaps you could sound out Mr. Blair about it when he comes here in a couple of days. And maybe a word with the Poles would not be amiss.

No-one can tell me why Tony's suddenly decided to come here again.

In Britain many believe he needs to see a friendly face, someone who is in the same boat as he is; others think he wants you to agree on a date to extricate yourselves from Iraq.

If that's so then he can save himself the trip.

Now, Sir, I must take my leave, I've got a plane to catch. You cannot imagine how I look forward to learning about the reaction to your re-election suggestion. And I wish you well in the mid-terms. Do you think there is any danger your party will lose?

Not a Chinaman's chance. Gee, I guess I'm not supposed to say that any more. But you'll be one of the first to know about my re-election suggestion and the mid-terms.

With all you've taught me about how the Brits talk at least I'll be able to understand Tony a bit better on his upcoming visit. I'm sorry you've got to go but maybe when I see you again it will be at my next inauguration. There are an awful lot of guys getting' ready to run but I don't think they can say no to a president, can they?

Certainly not, Sir. No-one should be able to take precedent over a president.

I must remember that in case anyone objects. Now I better call Jeb, just in case he's still got ideas. So long and good luck down south.

Goodbye, Sir, and thank you again.

Abramoff, Jack .... Republican lobbyist serving time for
fraud and corrup-
tion.

Ahern, Bertie .... Irish Prime Minister.
Rumoured to have
been the interpreter
when he met with
US President George
W. Bush and UK
Prime Minister Tony
Blair in Northern Ire-
land on 8 April 2003.

Annan, Kofi................ Former United Nations Secretary Gen-
eral, the first U.N.
staff member to
hold the post.

Ashcroft, John........... United States Attor-
ney General 2001-
2005. His greatest
distinction is that he
lost the election for
a U.S. Senate seat to
a dead man.

Aznar, José
María .... Prime Minister of
Spain 1996-2004. His
habit of jumping to

conclusions cost him the 2004 general election.

Berlusconi, Silvio .... Prime Minister of Italy 2001-2006. Media proprietor and composer of Neapolitan love songs. Re-elected in 2008.

Black Jack .... General "Black Jack" John Joseph Pershing, U.S. Army General who died in 1948.

Blair, Cherie .... Wife of Tony Blair and high-ranking English Queen's Counsel barrister (a lawyer who wears a wig).

Blair, Tony .... Prime Minister of the United Kingdom for ten years. Best known for always being sincere, even when telling what London's Cockneys call "pork pies".

Blunkett, David .... Former British Home (Interior) Secretary. Forced to resign when his affair with a married woman became public. The paternity suit did not help.

Bremer, Paul .... Head of the Iraq Coalition Provisional Authority, better known as George Bush's Pro-Consul.

Bush, George W. .... Forty-third president of the United States. Took office in 2000 when the U.S. Supreme Court agreed with the Florida Supreme Court decision to appoint him as president. In 2001 he authorized a US$1.35 billion tax cut for the rich saying it would stimulate the economy and provide more jobs. Elected in 2004 he converted a 2000 US$86 billion budget surplus into a multi-billion dollar budget deficit demonstrating, according to Treasury Secretary Henry Paulson "the remarkable strength of the U.S. economy."

Bush, Jeb .... President George Bush's brother and two-term Governor of Florida. Fixed things so his brother could become president in 2000.

Butler, Lord................. British career civil servant who headed enquiry into intelligence on non-existent weapons of mass destruction that led to Iraq war.

Cameron, David ...... Leader of the British Conservative (Tory) Party. An English toff who tries to pass himself off as a pleb.

Campbell,
  Alastair .... Tony Blair's former Director of Communications and Strategy and Chief Spinner.

Chavez, Linda........... Appointed Secretary of Labour by Bush but nomination withdrawn after confessing she employed an illegal immigrant as a nanny.

Cheney, Dick .... U.S. Vice President: From 1995 to 2000 Chairman and Chief Executive Officer of Halliburton, the company that has made, and makes, billions of dollars from the Iraq war, some for services never provided.

Chirac, Jacques .... Former President of France. Under investigation because of alleged financial improprieties while Mayor of Paris.

Conrad Black,
  Lord .... Canadian newspaper proprietor who changed his nationality to British. Sentenced in Chicago for misappropriating

millions of dollars from his newspaper empire.

Cunningham,
Randy Duke........... U.S. Republican Congressman from California who re-signed after admit-ting he accepted bribes.

Davies, Ray .... Co-founder of the English rock group The Kinks.

Davis,
Dr. Raymond .... Co-winner of the Nobel Prize for Phys-ics.

DeLay,
Thomas (Tom)........... U.S. Republican Party House of Rep-resentatives Majority Leader 2003–2005. Indicted by a Texas grand jury on crimi-nal charges for con-spiring to violate campaign finance laws.

Dobbs, Lou .... American television and radio business reporter. Hates immigrants, especially Mexicans, and says private Minutemen should control the border. Some wonder whether he has not noticed his wife is Mexican-American.

Dole, Bob.................... Former U.S. Senator and presidential candidate who extolled the virtues of Viagra on television.

Fabian Society.......... Socialist Society affiliated to the British Labour Party.

Foggo, Kyle .... Former U.S. government intelligence officer charged with fraud and other offenses.

Gerry, Elbridge.......... Long ago Governor of Massachusetts who gave the name to gerrymandering, or redistricting, to manipulate electoral boundaries.

Gingrich, Newt .... Former Republican Speaker of the U.S.

House of Repre-
sentatives. Married
three times, was
having an illicit affair
while criticizing Bill
Clinton about Moni-
ca Lewinsky.

Giuliani, Rudy .... Former Mayor of
New York. Married
three times. It was
18 years before
he noticed his first
wife was his sec-
ond cousin. As he
wanted to marry
someone else, the
Catholic Church an-
nulled the marriage.

Gore, Al .... Former U.S. Vice
President and cam-
paigner against glo-
bal warming. When
it was announced
he was writing An
Inconvenient Truth
some thought it was
about the 2000 gen-
eral election rather
than about climate
change.

Goss, Porter .... Former CIA Director. Sept.2004-May 2006. Suddenly resigned with no explanation. He later said his res-ignation was "just one of those myster-ies".

Halliburton .... Company of which Vice President Dick Cheney was C.E.O. and makes billions of dollars from the Iraq war.

Henman, Tim .... British Tennis Player. Honoured for his ability to reach Wimbleton semi-fi-nals.

Hodge, Margaret ..... British Labour politi-cian who held minis-terial posts.

Howard, Michael ...... Former leader of the British Conservative (Tory) Party.

Hutton, Lauren .... American actress and model. Best known for her gap-toothed smile.

Hutton,
  Lord Brian .... British law lord who
                          headed the inquiry
                          into the death of
                          Dr. David Kelly.
Joyce, James .... Irish writer and poet
                          best known for Ul-
                          ysses and Finnegans
                          Wake. Had almost
                          as much influence
                          on the English lan-
                          guage as President
                          Bush.
Kelly, Dr. David .... Biological warfare
                          expert and former
                          U.N. weapons in-
                          spector in Iraq.
                          Questioned the
                          U.K. government's
                          "dodgy dossier"
                          about non-existing
                          weapons of mass
                          destruction. Was
                          found dead near his
                          home in England.
                          His death was de-
                          clared a suicide.
Kenny Boy .... Kenneth Lay.
Kerik, Bernard............ Rudy Giuliani pro-
                          tégé and New York
                          City Police Com-

missioner. George Bush nominated him as Secretary of Homeland Security but Kerik withdrew with the excuse that he had employed an illegal immigrant as a nanny. Under indictment for conspiracy, mail fraud, wire fraud and lying to the Internal Revenue Service.

King, Larry.................. American television talk show host. He invites those under indictment to come on his show and assure viewers they are innocent.

Kombo, Dr. Ernest..... An African Jesuit, Bishop of Owando in the Congo. Told a meeting of bishops in Rome, attended by Pope John Paul, the College of Cardinals should be expanded to include women.

Kostyra, Martha .... Martha Stewart.

Lay, Kenneth............. American business-
man and C.E.O.
of Enron. Indicted
and found guilty of
multiple counts of
securities fraud. His
death shortly be-
fore he was to be
sentenced meant
the proceeds of his
crimes were not re-
paid.

Lay, Linda .... Kenneth Lay's wife.

Livingstone,
  Kenneth .... "Red Ken", Mayor of
London. "Red" does
not refer to his hair
colour.

Lott, Trent................... Former U.S. senator
criticised for cham-
pioning Strom Thur-
mond, South Caro-
lina Senator and
racial segregationist.

Murdoch, Rupert ..... Australian global
media tycoon who
changed nation-
alities to get into
the U.S. market.
Rumoured to have

tried to do the same to get into the Chinese market.

Negroponte,
John .... U.S. Deputy Secretary of State, son of a Greek shipping magnate. Has had a less than stellar diplomatic career.

Perry, Fred .... English tennis player. Wimbleton champion in the 1930s.

Pershing, General..... Black Jack.

Portillo, Michael .... British Conservative (Tory) politician, once thought to be a future Party leader.

Prescott, John........... Former British Deputy Prime Minister. Had an affair with a staff member to which no-one objected until it was discovered he was using his office as a love nest.

Prestowitz, Clyde ...... Founder and President of the Economic Strategy Institute.

Served as counselor to the Secretary of Commerce in the Reagan Administration.

Quinn, Kimberly......... American journalist, commentator, and magazine publisher, including The Spectator a British magazine. While married – to someone else – had an affair and a child with British Labour Home Secretary David Blunkett.

Rice,
  Condoleezza......... U.S. Secretary of State who likes to talk a lot but manages to say very little.

Ridge, Tom .... First U.S Secretary of Homeland Security, 2003-2005.

Roberts, John............Chief Justice of the U.S. appointed by President Bush.

Rove, Karl .... Resigned as Deputy Chief of Staff to President Bush. Retired

Ambassador Joseph Wilson claimed Rove leaked the identity of his wife, Valerie Plame, as a covert Central Intelligence Agency (CIA) agent.

Rumsfeld, Donald ....Former U.S. Secretary of defence. Hailed as a second Einstein by some because of his discovery of the new Universal Law of Stuff Happens.

Schwarzenneger, Arnold ....Austrian bodybuilder and now Governor of California.

Short, Clare ....British Labour Party politician who left the Party over differences about the Iraq war to become an Independent Member of Parliament.

Snow, John................ Former U.S, Treasury Secretary who predicted: "the president's [George

Bush] legacy will be one of having significantly reduced the deficit in his time".

Snow, Tony .... Former U.S. presidential Press Secretary. Long time Fox news commentator. Classified President Bush, before his appointment, as "an embarrassment" and "impotent".

Sopranos .... U.S. soap opera about a New Jersey crime family's trials, tribulations and triumphs.

Stewart, Martha........ TV homemaking expert sentenced to prison and probation for lying to investigators about her sale of stock.

Straw, Jack .... British Labour Party politician and former Foreign Secretary. Became so friendly with Secretary of State Rice that, when travelling in

her aircraft, she let
him sleep in her bed
(she was not in it).

Walesa, Lech .... Former President of
Poland.

Williams, Dr. Rowan .. Archbishop of Canterbury and head of
the Church of Eng-
land.

Woodward, Bob .... Washington Post assistant editor and
Watergate journalist.
Now spends most
of his time writing
blockbusters and
pontificating.

Woodward,
   Sir Clive................... English rugby player.
Knighted when the
England Rugby
team won a game.

Zapatero,
   José Luis .... Spanish Prime Minister. Won the gen-
eral election in 2004
when his opponent
blamed the wrong
people for the Ma-
drid train bombings.

874050

Made in the USA